911·1

English # Heritage

Book of

Stonehenge

English ⌗ Heritage
Book of
Stonehenge

Julian Richards

B. T. Batsford Ltd/English Heritage
London

Typeset by
Lasertext Ltd., Thomas Street, Stretford,
Manchester M32 0JT
and printed in Great Britain by
The Bath Press, Bath, Avon

Published by
B. T. Batsford Ltd
4 Fitzhardinge Street,
London W1H 0AH

A CIP catalogue record for this book is
available from the British Library

ISBN 0 7134 6141 1 (cased)
0 7134 6142 X (limp)

Contents

Illustrations

Colour plates

Acknowledgements

The information on which this book is largely based is derived from the results of the Stonehenge Environs Project, undertaken while I worked for the Trust for Wessex Archaeology. This project was mostly funded by English Heritage, with additional support from the National Trust, the British Academy, the Society of Antiquaries of London, the Prehistoric Society and the Wiltshire Library and Museums Service. I would like to thank all the individual fieldworkers and specialists whose efforts made the project and its publication possible.

In preparing this book Stephen Johnson, Peter Kemmis Betty and Sarah Vernon-Hunt have all offered sound editorial advice, despite which I trust that sufficient of my idiosyncrasies have survived.

For illustrative material I would like to thank the following:

Jane Brayne for the majority of the reconstruction drawings (7, 8, 9, 16, 34, 35, 56, 61, 76, 80, 83, 89, 99, 103, and colour plates 3, 4, 5, 10, 11. All copyright Wessex Archaeology).

Colour plate 12 by Jane Brayne is copyright Jane Brayne.
Linda Coleman (12, 14, 49, 50, 77, 78, 93, 100 and 101)
Julian Cross (15, 17 (part), 85 and 96)
Serena Garrett (102)
Elizabeth James (84)
Robert Read (3, 5, 6, 59, 63, 68, 74, 75, 91 and 108)
Miranda Schofield (70 and 98)

The aerial photographs (18, 32, 48, 57, 87, 88 and colour plate 6) are by kind permission of Mick Aston. 29 is by kind permission of the RCHM.

The engraving (23), photograph (25) and colour plate 12 are by kind permission of the Wiltshire Archaeological and Natural History Society.

With the exception of 4 (Elaine Wakefield), 10 (Sue Lobb) 27 (Austin Underwood) and 28 (Sue Davies) remaining photographs are by Julian Richards.

31, 51, 82, 104 and colour plates 1, 2, 7, 8 and 9 are by kind permission of English Heritage.

—— 1 ——
In sight of Stonehenge

For many centuries, since written records have preserved thoughts, ideas and opinions, Stonehenge (1) has been many different things to many different people. The same is true today. Some would see it as a monument to the victims of historic battles, to others it is a solar-powered calculator, or a temple as alive today as when it was first built. For many though, the constant function of Stonehenge is as a magnet, not literally, but attracting both interest and speculation; and also past antiquarians and present archaeologists, all of whom have combined to contribute to a rich written and visual record of a unique monument. This book does not set out to review this copious iconography; that has already been done in a book (perhaps optimistically) entitled *Stonehenge Complete*. Neither does it set out simply to be a guide, although it is hoped that it may act as an encouragement to exploration.

1 *Stonehenge today; unique and enigmatic.*

What it does set out to do is to re-examine Stonehenge in the context of our current understanding of both the monument itself, and of the surrounding prehistoric landscape. Here, over several thousand years, ditches were dug, mounds raised and stones transported and lifted in an enduring demonstration of communal effort and faith. This book will illustrate the development of this landscape and our developing understanding of its creators and users.

The stimulus for this reappraisal of an admittedly much studied landscape and monument lies in the considerable body of both fieldwork and analysis that have been carried out during the last decade. The richness of the prehistoric landscape that surrounds Stonehenge has long been acknowledged, but has been reinforced by the results of two major recent landscape projects. Initially the Royal Commission on the Historic Monuments of England mapped those components of the prehistoric landscape that survived on the ground. To this framework was added the extra dimension, revealed by aerial photography, of sites never before seen, levelled by ploughing before the earliest archaeologists looked out into the Stonehenge landscape. Following on from this study, published in 1979 under the title of *Stonehenge and its Environs*, the Trust for Wessex Archaeology between 1980 and 1984 carried out a major programme of survey and excavation. Known but ill-understood sites were examined, excavation providing evidence not only for dating, but also for function and the changing prehistoric environment. More importantly, for the first time, large areas of the landscape were systematically searched for traces of settlement and everyday activities, evidence for the lives of the people who had built and used the great complex of monuments surrounding Stonehenge. This investigation has provided the greatest insight into the lives of those who have been called the 'Stonehenge people'. Now too, the results of important sites excavated during previous decades have for the first time been made fully available. Work is still in progress on the analysis of the excavations carried out at Stonehenge itself, but sufficient is now understood to allow the complex development of this monument to be placed in the context of the wider prehistoric landscape.

To enter the ranks of those who have written about Stonehenge is to step into an arena where, apparently, none fear to tread. Books, papers, reviews and letters emerge in a continuous stream, written from many differing viewpoints but all with the same air of conviction and authority. Some offer a reasoned personal alternative to traditional archaeological dogma; others views that can only be described as bizarre, in which even the basic framework of our prehistoric chronology is overwhelmed in a tide of mysticism. It is consequently almost mandatory for newcomers to these ranks to state not only their credentials, but also their manifesto, the vision of Stonehenge from which they intend to proceed.

This author is first and foremost an archaeologist; a pragmatic prehistorian with a genuine affection for Stonehenge and a great respect for its builders and users. These feelings stem from a decade of involvement with Stonehenge and its landscape, during which time a variety of experiences have inevitably produced a sense of intimacy with the prehistoric past. Pragmatism dictates that ley lines and earth forces will play no part in this discussion while aspects of astronomy and mathematics have been firmly placed in chapter 11: 'Stonehenge – beyond the evidence'. It is true that these aspects deserve a more lengthy interrogation than that which is possible in a book of this length, and also that this author is far from qualified to provide the necessary critical approach. However, their relegation to this chapter, alongside less credible elements of the Stonehenge mythology, represents a positive attempt to separate fact from fiction.

2

The Stonehenge environs

The monument of Stonehenge has lent its name to a number of more abstract concepts: the 'Age of Stonehenge' and the elusive 'Stonehenge People', although where the surrounding 'Stonehenge landscape' is concerned, a more established concept exists. This book will examine an area known as the 'Stonehenge Environs', the boundaries of which were established, mapped and published by the Wiltshire antiquary Sir Richard Colt Hoare in the early part of the nineteenth century (2). In his *Ancient History of Wiltshire*, published in 1812, he used the term to delineate the rich archaeological landscape surrounding Stonehenge, a landscape remarkable for both the composition and the density of the monuments it encloses. The

2 *Sir Richard Colt Hoare's map of Stonehenge and its Environs published in 1812.*

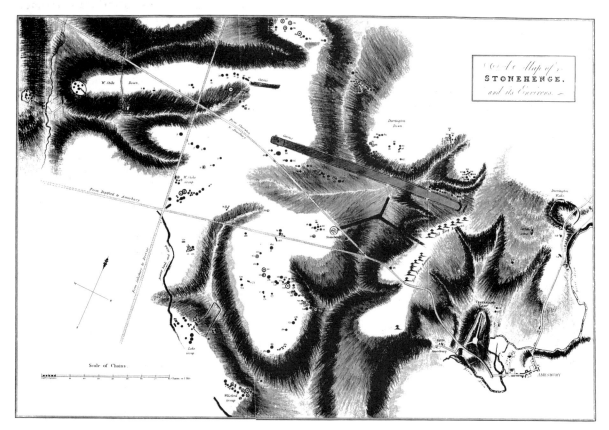

concept of these 'Environs', the wider setting for Stonehenge as defined by Colt Hoare, if not their precise boundaries, has been employed by both the major landscape studies that have been carried out in this area during the 1980s.

The physical setting

Stonehenge and its Environs are situated on the undulating chalk of Salisbury Plain about 13 km (8 miles) north of Salisbury and close to the small town of Amesbury (3). The easterly boundary of the Environs is effectively formed by the valley of the River Avon, at the edge of which lie Amesbury to the south and the henge monument of Durrington Walls to the north. To the west, the valley of the much smaller River Till forms the boundary, while to the north and south the absence of such topographic features means that defined boundaries are inevitably more subjective. The southerly extent is generally taken to be marked by the Wilsford barrow group and the topographically, if not archaeologically, prominent Rox Hill. This is the hill on which the clump of trees, viewed from Stonehenge, resembles to those with a good imagination a galleon in sail. The northern boundary is less easily defined, and for the purposes of recent studies has been extended beyond the area originally defined by Colt Hoare in order to include the causewayed enclosure of Robin Hood's Ball.

The geology of the area is entirely of Middle Chalk, ranging in height from between 130m (430 ft) OD on the gentle downland crests to a little over 60m (200 ft) OD in the valleys of the Avon and the Till. Despite this apparent geological uniformity the chalk varies considerably, from hard and rock-like in areas such as the King Barrow Ridge to the west of the Avon Valley, to soft and considerably disturbed by periglacial action to the west of Stonehenge. Here small clay pockets and solution features of varying shapes make the chalk surface irregular and subject to widely differing weathering.

In the area between the river valleys the chalk is largely devoid of any capping of superficial deposits such as clay-with-flints, and is bisected by one major dry valley system. Close to Stonehenge this is, hardly surprisingly, known as Stonehenge Bottom, and here its profile, with a wide, flat valley floor suggests the possibility of deep accumulations of soil washed from the surrounding slopes during periods of past cultivation. Despite this appearance, an extensive campaign of research excavations, carried out in order to investigate such hillwash deposits, failed consistently to locate any. What remains uncertain is whether such deposits never formed, or whether, after accumulating, they were subsequently scoured out into the valley of the River Avon by seasonal water action. The latter suggestion may be

3 *Location map of the Stonehenge area.*

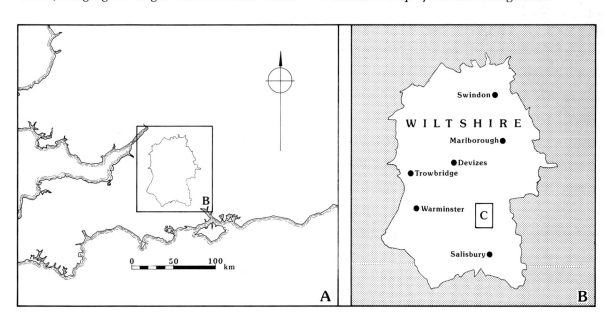

4 *The gently rolling chalk landscape of the Stonehenge Environs viewed from Wilsford Down. The barrow in the foreground is the Prophet Barrow, one of the Lake Barrow Group and the mounds of the Normanton Down Group can be seen in the middle distance. Bush Barrow is prominent under a clump of small trees.*

true as Stonehenge Bottom, which merges with Spring Bottom to the south before funnelling out into the valley of the River Avon at Wilsford-cum-Lake, has been recorded as flowing with water within living memory. In places the sides of this dry valley system are relatively steep, and form the only effective physical obstacle to present day arable cultivation. With the exception of these and similar slopes at the river valley margins, the gently undulating topography of the Stonehenge Environs is quite unremarkable in the context of Salisbury Plain as a whole (4).

The present day soils of the area are those characteristic of the chalklands, thin rendzinas which form over solid chalk or chalky drift deposits. Uncultivated soils, more widespread towards the interior of Salisbury Plain, where military training largely replaces agriculture,

now remain only on steeper slopes and in areas of long-standing pasture around some of the major monuments. The remaining soils, some of which have been in cultivation for several centuries, have all in consequence suffered a serious loss of humic material, compounded in some areas by the relative steepness of cultivated slopes. It is clear from the study of present-day soils that they are merely the remnants of those that originally existed within the Stonehenge area. Comparison with prehistoric soils, preserved for example by burial under earth mounds, demonstrates that there has been a considerable loss of fine soil components such as Loess (a wind-blown soil) over the past three or four thousand years. Once extensive deposits of clay-with-flints, important for soil generation, can also be demonstrated as having been almost totally destroyed by cultivation. Simply looking at the present-day soils, it is hard to believe that the chalklands could have attracted early farmers, despite the relative ease of clearance, cultivation and drainage. It is easier to understand when the degree of loss is calculated, and some idea can be gained of the potential fertility of the soils

5 *Map of the Stonehenge Environs.*

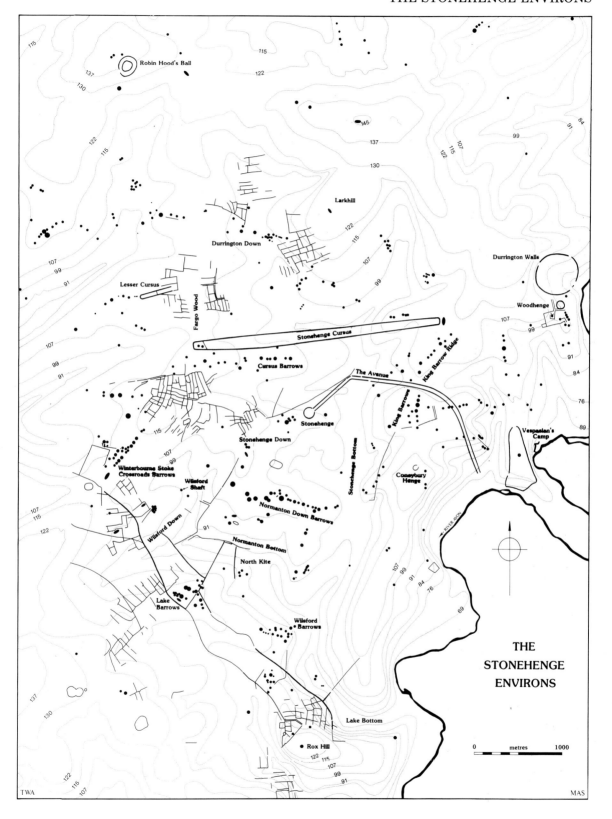

Robin Hood's Ball

Larkhill

Durrington Down

Durrington Walls

Lesser Cursus

Fargo Wood

Woodhenge

Stonehenge Cursus

King Barrow Ridge

Cursus Barrows

The Avenue

King Barrows

Stonehenge

Vespasian's Camp

Stonehenge Down

King Barrow

Stonehenge Bottom

Coneybury Henge

Winterbourne Stoke Crossroads Barrows

Wilsford Shaft

Normanton Down Barrows

Wilsford Down

RIVER AVON

Normanton Bottom

North Kite

Lake Barrows

Wilsford Barrows

THE
STONEHENGE
ENVIRONS

Lake Bottom

Rox Hill

0   metres   1000

TWA   MAS

17

that washed or blew away during early phases of cultivation. Contemporary farming methods restore a transient fertility to the thin surviving soils, but the fertility that drew the early farmers can never be replaced.

The prehistoric monuments, a brief description and chronology

Topographically the Stonehenge area is unremarkable; its configuration of small rivers, undulating through a landscape of gently-rounded hills and coombes could be duplicated many times over within the chalklands of southern England. However, within this physically undistinguished area lies the densest and most varied complex of Neolithic and Bronze Age monuments in southern England, and perhaps in western Europe (5). Together, these monuments demonstrate an intensity of prehistoric activity paralleled only within the Wessex chalklands in the Avebury area and on the south-east Dorset Ridgeway. In contrast to these areas, however, the Stonehenge Environs

exhibit a greater diversity of monuments, some unique, which clearly demonstrate that even the earliest phase of Stonehenge was constructed in a landscape already of considerable ceremonial and funerary significance.

The monuments within the Stonehenge area, their dates and associated changes in ceramic style are shown in chronological order in 6. The majority of these monuments belong to the Neolithic (New Stone Age) period (c.4000 – c. 2000 BC) or to the succeeding Bronze Age (c.2000 – c.800 BC). These periods should be regarded only as broad divisions of prehistoric time, their beginnings and ends not marked by events such as invasion or dynastic change. Innovations such as metal, which is one traditional mark of period transition, arrived gradually, first to the wealthy and powerful,

6 *A table of monuments, dates and pottery styles for the Stonehenge Environs.*

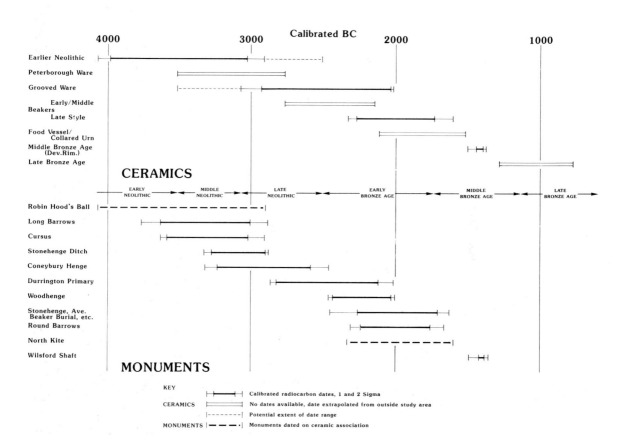

7 *Woodland clearance in the Early Neolithic. The use of axes of chipped and ground stone to fell trees produces a tapering profile on the upper part of the trunk while the lower stump becomes more ragged (Jane Brayne).*

their effects spreading slowly throughout society in general. The evidence for dating is provided by association, for example with types of pottery or other artefacts of known date, or more directly, by such means as radiocarbon dating. This technique, involving the measurement of radioactive carbon isotopes present in all living matter, produces dates which require calibration before they can be expressed as calendar years. For the purposes of this book, all dates have been calibrated and are expressed in calendar years (years BC, but see Glossary for a more complete explanation of radiocarbon dating).

The very beginning of the Neolithic period witnessed a revolution, perhaps initially small in scale, in the subsistence patterns practised in this country. Britain had been an island for a relatively short time in geological terms, the rising waters caused by the last melting of the glacial ice having cut off the land links with the continent in about 8000 BC. On this new island, as before, mobile Mesolithic (Middle Stone Age) communities hunted, fished and gathered wild foods, each adapting to the resources available within their loosely-defined territory. The degree of mobility of these communities was largely dictated by the stability of their food resources. In areas where food and other essential commodities such as stone for tools, water and wood, were abundant then settlement on at least a semi-permanent or

seasonal basis was possible. It is in circumstances such as these that the first evidence for modification of the natural landscape can be seen. Embarking on a course that would inevitably have resulted in the independent development of agriculture, indications can be seen in the vegetational record of the small-scale clearance of woodland, possibly by fire. The results of this would be quickly seen in the proliferation of colonizing species such as hazel, far more useful for the nuts they produced than the trees of the natural unmodified woodland.

Such change was, however, gradual, and was far from extensive in its effects, even in areas where much evidence for Mesolithic communities can be seen. A dramatic, if not instantaneous change was to take place only on the introduction of farming, which finally arrived in Britain after a slow spread across Europe from its origins in the Near East. Alongside the communities of hunters and gatherers the first farmers cleared areas for cultivation (7) and planted cereals that through human interference over thousands of years had slowly evolved from wild grasses. The other newly introduced aspect of farming, the very precious

8 *A Neolithic earthen long barrow, the gradually tapering mound flanked by quarry ditches (Jane Brayne).*

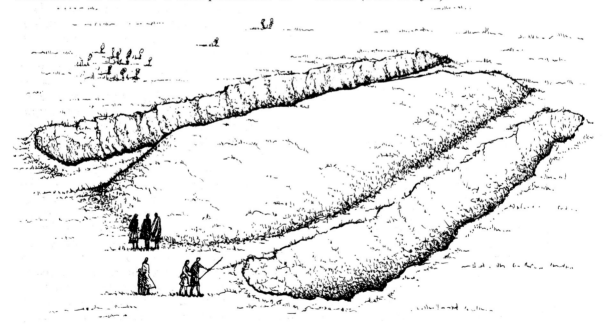

domesticated animals, were no doubt carefully protected from their wild counterparts during this pioneering phase. One of the most dramatic effects of the gradual spread of this revolution was to tie former wanderers to a patch of land made special through the investment of their labour. This must surely have been responsible for the rapid development of the concept of territory and of ownership of land which, once established, required regular reinforcement. In a land without boundaries it is possible that attempts were made to substantiate territorial claims by calling on the power of ancestors, whose presence could be made tangible through the new potential for communal effort. Agriculture, by requiring effort in clearing, planting, weeding, crop protection and harvesting, binds people not only to the selected area of land, but also to an annual cycle. Unlike the cycle practised by hunters and gatherers which, while often incorporating the exploitation of seasonally available resources, involved year round activity, the agricultural cycle may include potentially slack or free time. At such times, when the efforts of the community were not required for food production, communal construction tasks could be carried out. The earliest results of such communal effort in the Stonehenge area and in much of southern Britain can be seen in the long barrows which, together with causewayed enclosures, represent the first broad phase of monument construction.

Long barrows, elongated mounds often with wide flanking ditches from which the material to construct the mound was quarried (8), may simply be tombs. Many excavated examples have been found to contain multiple burials, some within mortuary 'houses' constructed either of wood or of stone. Others, however, despite extensive excavation, appear never to have contained any burials, and indeed, may never have been intended to act as receptacles for the dead. It is possible that such mounds were constructed as cenotaphs, memorials to absent dead with no outward indications that they were empty. It is equally possible that they were intended to act as a physical claim to an area of land. Silhouetted against a skyline, at the edge of an area of cleared and farmed land, the long barrow would make an impressive title deed, warning potential interlopers that the occupiers of that land had done so for some considerable time. Whether or not the tomb contained the proof in the form of the ancestral bones was presumably not something that would be investigated by rival claimants.

Causewayed enclosures, constructed later in the Early Neolithic, are found in a variety of situations, from flat valley floors to hilltops, and can be distinguished from later types of enclosure by the many entrances in their irregular circuits of ditches and banks. Single, double, or multiple circuits consist of short and often haphazardly dug sections of ditch, generally mirrored by lengths of bank placed on the interior side, together giving the appearance of two parallel strings of sausages. Such enclosures, of which Robin Hood's Ball to the north-west of Stonehenge (see **59** and p.73) is a well-preserved example, may have functioned in a variety of ways according to the needs of the communities that built and used them. Although the numerous entrances appear to render the enclosures useless for defensive purposes, some, for example Crickley Hill in Gloucestershire and part of the great complex on Hambledon Hill in Dorset, may have fulfilled a defensive function. Excavation at these two commandingly-positioned sites has provided evidence for both strong defences, in the form of ramparts of earth and stone, and for the attack and destruction of these defences. At both sites scatters of flint arrowheads were found concentrated around entrances, shown by excavation to be defended gateways. This points to concerted attack; the ditch at Hambledon Hill even contained the skeleton of a 'defender', flint arrowheads still embedded in his bones. A similarly defensive function is unlikely in the case of Robin Hood's Ball, sited on a gently sloping ridge, and here a more economic or spiritual function must be sought.

The work carried out by Roger Mercer at Hambledon Hill represents the most extensive examination of the interior of a complex of causewayed enclosures and has provided evidence to suggest that at least part of the complex was used for funerary rites, including the exposure of corpses prior to burial. In many more cases, limited exploration of the ditches has been carried out, often revealing unusually dense deposits of animal bone. Such deposits have been interpreted as the remains of feasts and have given rise to one of the more enduring and popular explanations of the role of causewayed enclosures: as ceremonial meeting

9 *Ditch digging in the Neolithic period. Before the use of metal, picks of red deer antler made effective tools for loosening up hard chalk. Bone shovels and baskets were probably used for shifting the resulting rubble (Jane Brayne).*

places for trade, feasting and celebration.

The construction of causewayed enclosures and long barrows has been suggested as representing a response to the stresses of a 'pioneering' phase of the Early Neolithic. An alternative viewpoint suggests that their construction represents a period of stabilization and consolidation, and may therefore not represent the very earliest phase of this period.

The scale of the construction of these monuments is an impressive indication of both the power of social cohesion, and of tools of wood, bone and antler when combined with human effort. Ditches were dug using picks of red deer antler and corresponding mounds were raised, we assume, by carting the loosened spoil either in skins or in baskets (**9**). The picks are very effective even when digging in hard chalk and, contrary to the usually quoted evidence, do not

need to be hammered in and then used to lever out lumps of chalk. Experiment has shown that they are very effective when used in the same way as a modern pick, swung hard at the chalk to break up the surface (**10**). One aspect of antler picks that is not generally appreciated is that according to the side of the animal's head from which the antler came, the curvature of the first, or brow tine (the pick blade) will vary. This makes some picks only useable by right-handed diggers and others by those who are left-handed.

Whatever their exact place in the chronological order of the earlier Neolithic, these monuments form our most tangible link with the farming communities of this period. Their distribution throughout the landscape has led to the identification of developing territories, territories within which, however, almost nothing is known about patterns of everyday life, settlement and the wider exploitation of the landscape. In terms of artefacts, both the monuments described above and areas of contemporary settlement are associated with the first pottery to be found in this country, and by forms of flint tools unlike those of the preceding Mesolithic period.

The majority of the pots produced during the earlier Neolithic were made of locally obtained clay, a conclusion reached by the careful study of the natural components of the clay: sands and larger particles such as fragments of fossil shell. As demonstrated clearly by the manner in which these pots fracture, they were formed mainly by the process of coil building, although some may have been slab-built, and smaller vessels may have simply been pinched out of a ball of clay. The forms produced by these processes of hand-building were round-bottomed, rather baggy, possibly reflecting the shape of more common organic containers such as skin bags or wicker baskets. At first they are rarely decorated except for occasional patches of surface burnishing, smoothing carried out with a hard object when the pot is in a partly dry 'leather hard' state. With the exception of pierced lugs, added for the purpose of suspension, these pots, fired in an open bonfire rather than in a deliberately constructed kiln (11) have few distinguishing features (12). Alongside the local products, pots of

a type of clay which can only have come from the Lizard area in Cornwall are occasionally found, most commonly within causewayed enclosures. Such 'gabbroic ware' pots, fragile commodities to be carried over such great distances, provide a clear indication of developing networks of trade and communication.

Within the groups of worked flint which form such an important part of the surviving material culture of the Neolithic period, considerable changes can now be observed. With the exception of chipped axes, much of the toolkit of the Mesolithic hunter-gatherers was designed to be light, portable and economic, with a raw material which might not always be readily available. Long flint blades, produced by a systematic and very controlled flint knapping technique, provided cutting tools and the

10 *Experimental digging using antler picks. Using fresh antler picks the hole in the photograph was dug by two people in less than a day. A hole this size would have held one of the great wooden posts at Durrington Walls.*

11 *Experimental bonfire firing of replica Neolithic pottery. Sand, flint, crushed pottery or organic matter need to be added to clay to help pots withstand the sharp changes of temperature found in such uncontrolled firing conditions.*

basis for the manufacture of microliths, tiny finely-worked points used as arrow barbs or mounted in wooden hafts to form composite cutting tools. As life became more settled during the Neolithic period the production of blades declines, replaced by more robust flakes and flake tools. Other changes include the grinding smooth of some axes after initial shaping and the replacement of composite barbed arrowhead forms with fine one-piece leaf-shaped arrowheads (**13**).

As suggested by **6**, the middle of the Neolithic period is a time which sees the gradual disappearance of certain types of monument and styles of pottery, and their gradual replacement by novel forms. Long barrows reach their final stage of development, often becoming shorter

and with 'U' shaped ditches that encircle one end of the mound. Although limited, the excavation evidence from such 'short' long barrows points to a change in burial practice, from multiple to individual burial. The wider implications of this change in social and economic terms will be seen in a more developed form at the very end of the Neolithic period. While some long barrows are becoming shorter, other types of monument, also possibly developed from the same original concept, are reaching extreme lengths. In parts of Dorset in particular the long barrow finds its ultimate expression in the form of bank barrows, elongated mounds of which perhaps the best-known example is the one within the hillfort of Maiden Castle near Dorchester. More widespread are cursus monuments: here the original form of the long barrow appears to have been greatly extended to produce a massively elongated ditched enclosure, lacking any vestiges of a central long mound. Despite investigation, the function of such monuments, of which there are two examples within the Stonehenge Environs, is still far from certain, although they may best be regarded as fulfilling a ceremonial, possibly processional function.

Within the developing ceramic traditions, and associated with the monuments described above, the decoration first seen on the earlier Ebbsfleet Ware finds greater expression in the various elaborate Peterborough styles of pottery (**14**). Decoration is both extensive and exuberant, with both the exterior and interior of the pots often covered with complex designs in which impressed motifs, using bone or twisted cord, play an important part.

This middle Neolithic period has sometimes been viewed as a hiatus, a period of stagnation, within which the construction of monuments is at a relative standstill and the early agricultural enclosures lie neglected and overgrown. This does not seem to be the case within the Stonehenge Environs where the construction of communal monuments appears to carry on apace within what was an increasingly utilized landscape.

Robin Hood's Ball causewayed enclosure, over a dozen long barrows, and the two cursus monuments all pre-date Stonehenge, where construction of the first phase, a simple earthwork enclosure, commenced in around 2800 BC. This early, and at this stage almost insignificant Stonehenge appears to have been used for

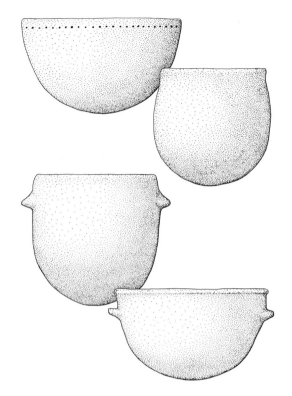

12 *Early Neolithic pottery forms: simple, round-bottomed pots with little decoration (after Gibson).*

unifying characteristics can also be identified. Some, such as the orientation of their entrances, suggest widely held religious beliefs and a willingness to invest huge communal effort in their physical manifestation. These changes in both styles of pottery and in forms of monuments are also matched in the range of flint tools now produced (**15**), some of which, particularly certain types of 'transverse' arrowheads were clearly never intended for use and as such must be viewed as prestige items.

The changes in economy and subsistence which occurred at the beginning of the Neolithic laid the foundations for a period during which an apparently egalitarian society developed. Within southern Britain the graves of individuals are rare, and in stark contrast to the magnificent 'public' works into which so much effort is concentrated. Towards the end of this period a change occurs: individual power and wealth become possible as new prestige items in the form of copper tools and weapons and fine Beaker pottery are introduced (**16**). Also part of this Beaker 'package' is archery

13 *Early Neolithic flint tool types: ground axes and leaf-shaped arrowheads.*

only a short while, its abandonment and decay marking the beginning of a recognizable Late Neolithic.

Within most of the British Isles the Late Neolithic can be characterized as a period of excess. Styles of pottery such as Peterborough Ware and Grooved Ware now develop even more elaborate decoration (see **14**) matched by the construction of a range of ceremonial monuments, some on a massive scale. These include avenues and circles of both stone and timber, huge earth mounds such as Silbury Hill near Avebury and, perhaps most typically in Wessex, henge monuments. These enclosures exemplified by sites such as Avebury and, within the Stonehenge Environs, Durrington Walls, Woodhenge and Coneybury (see **75, 77** and **78**), vary enormously in the scale and complexity of their construction. In simple terms henges are enclosures, their ditches often deep and lying inside the encircling bank. The central enclosed area frequently incorporates circular settings of stone or timber, and other

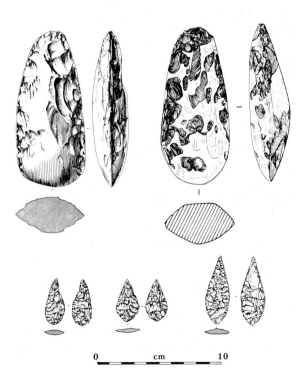

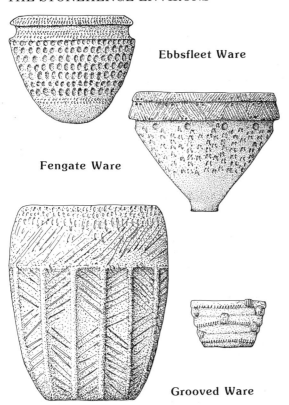

Ebbsfleet Ware

Fengate Ware

Grooved Ware

14 *Later Neolithic pottery styles: Peterborough and Grooved Ware (after Gibson).*

is altered, widened and extended in the form of the first stage of the Avenue while within the interior the major phase of construction in stone is started. The ruins which can be seen today are those of this great reconstruction, carried out over several centuries and paralleled by equally impressive developments in the surrounding landscape. On Wilsford Down to

15 *Later Neolithic flint tools: fabricators, a small and unusual type of axe and transverse arrowheads.*

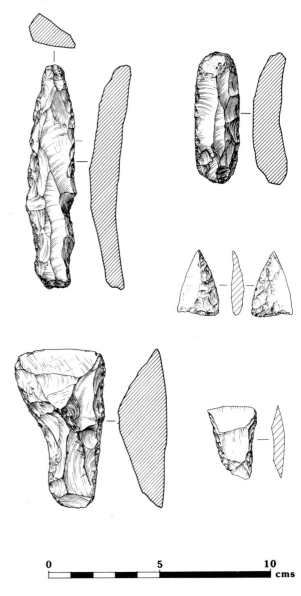

equipment, represented by flint arrowheads of barbed-and-tanged form and by archers' wrist-guards, flat perforated plates of stone designed to protect the inner arm from the sting of the bowstring (**17**). Power could be obtained by the control of such items, and the evidence of this power was often taken to the grave. Although the practice of burial beneath round mounds certainly started at an earlier date, this 'Beaker' period sees the almost universal adoption of the practice, with both inhumations and cremations now lying beneath mounds of circular form.

The evidence for individual wealth, provided by the rich grave goods which accompanied many of the burials, could perhaps be expected to mark the end of any concerted period of communal construction. This may be the case in many areas of Britain, but not at Stonehenge where the earlier and relatively insignificant earthwork enclosure is revived and remodelled after centuries of abandonment. The entrance the south of Stonehenge lies the North Kite (see p. 109), a large three-sided enclosure of the Beaker period and one of the area's unique monuments. On all sides of Stonehenge the individual and in many cases exceptionally large round barrows of the later Neolithic and early Bronze Age often formed the focus for the development throughout the Bronze Age of extensive barrow cemeteries. While the large mounds of the early bowl and bell barrows were carefully sited on the low crests of the downs in order to provide the maximum visual effect, it is more difficult to appreciate the true splendour of the lower disc, saucer and pond barrows (18). When explored in the early years of the nineteenth century, many of these 'fancy' barrows contained rich burials accompanied by weapons and tools of bronze, jewellery, amber, glass and gold. This richness led to the identification of a 'Wessex Culture', demonstrating the power of the individual and the regional supremacy of earlier Bronze Age Wessex.

Throughout the Middle Bronze Age, while Stonehenge was sporadically remodelled and the piecemeal extension of its Avenue continued, the barrow cemeteries also grew in extent and elaboration. Burials were added in and around existing barrow mounds, although there seems to be little evidence within the Stonehenge Environs for the extensive urnfield cremation cemeteries commonly found elsewhere within Wessex.

Although a decline in power and influence might be thought of as almost inevitable following such a long period of splendour, the later Bronze Age sees the development of an equally impressive, if more mundane landscape. Beyond Stonehenge and its protective cordon of barrow cemeteries aerial photography has revealed within the ploughed landscape extensive patterns of settlements, fields and boundaries. The agricultural landscape is organized into groups of small square 'Celtic' fields, in many cases linked to straggling boundary ditches which may represent a formalization of pre-existing territories. Such landscape features are notoriously difficult to date, but within the Stonehenge Environs the evidence for associated settlement, although limited, points to their origin in the Middle to Late Bronze Age.

During the subsequent Iron Age (c.800 BC – AD 43) there appears to be a genuine absence of activity over much of the Stonehenge Environs. The major exceptions are the substantial hillfort of Vespasian's Camp and the settlement discovered close to Durrington Walls, both of which lie adjacent to the River Avon. The pattern of settlement in surrounding and very similar areas suggests that this absence of settlement may be a true reflection of the very spiritual nature of the area, so obvious in the now crowded monumental landscape. In many ways this closing chapter of prehistory provides as great a contrast with surrounding areas of the Wessex chalk as do the spectacular concentrations of sites from the earlier prehistoric periods.

16 *The evidence of new ideas: highly-decorated Beaker pottery, weapons of copper and bronze and archery equipment (Jane Brayne).*

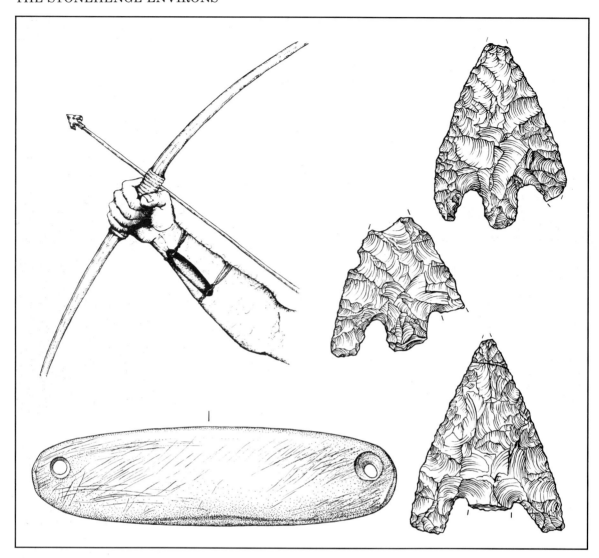

In order to introduce the story of the developing landscape, the preceding section has attempted to give some idea of the range and form of the component monuments, and of their function and chronology. The individual monuments, so briefly outlined here, will be described more fully within the chapters dealing with the overall development of the landscape in the different periods.

Reconstructing the past
In attempting to reconstruct the past, and particularly the remote past, it is essential to be aware of the limitations imposed by the available information on which all our interpretations must be founded. Many aspects

17 *Beaker period archery equipment. The stone wrist-guard protected the archer's arm against the sting of the bowstring (Jane Brayne). The wrist-guard and arrowheads from the burial in the Stonehenge ditch (Julian Cross).*

of the prehistoric past are lost to us for ever, including those which anthropologists find most helpful in their attempts to understand contemporary but comparable societies. Speech, the words which communicated the ideas that saw fruition in Stonehenge and other great monuments, cannot be recovered. Our sole physical contact with the builders of

18 *The complex barrow group at Winterbourne Stoke Crossroads. The Neolithic long barrow can be seen in the top left-hand corner, the alignment of its mound followed by the row of huge bowl and bell barrows. Beyond these lies a rare pond barrow and a pair of fragile disc barrows. Together these barrows represent nearly 2000 years of burial history (Mick Aston).*

Stonehenge is now with their dry bones (**19**); remains which provide few clues to their living appearance. Were the men clean shaven or bearded? (**colour plate 13**) were women conservatively dressed in neat homespun tunics, or tattooed from head to foot with decorative clothing and hair styles to match? The foundations of our understanding consist largely of the surviving parts of the material world, the built monuments, worked stones and fired pottery, which also provide the basis for some of our most fundamental chronologies. The objects and monuments in isolation cannot, however, provide us with insight into the world

of the 'Stonehenge People'; an understanding, often provided by anthropological study, of the place of such items within complex cultures is also required.

Evidence for change in both economy and the natural environment can be provided by a range of indicators such as animal bones, charcoals, seeds and snails, together with those that do not normally survive within dry chalk areas such as that surrounding Stonehenge. Organic materials, wood, leather and textiles, together with important environmental indicators such as pollen, insects and plant remains, do not usually survive the millennia in such conditions and have only ever been found in one, currently unique, deposit within the Stonehenge Environs.

This catalogue of loss by decay may seem pessimistic, but sufficient has survived and has been investigated, to enable the first confident attempts to be made at an understanding of the prehistoric past. This must encompass not merely the development of a landscape, but also the changing lives of those whose efforts, if not their physical appearance, remain visible

29

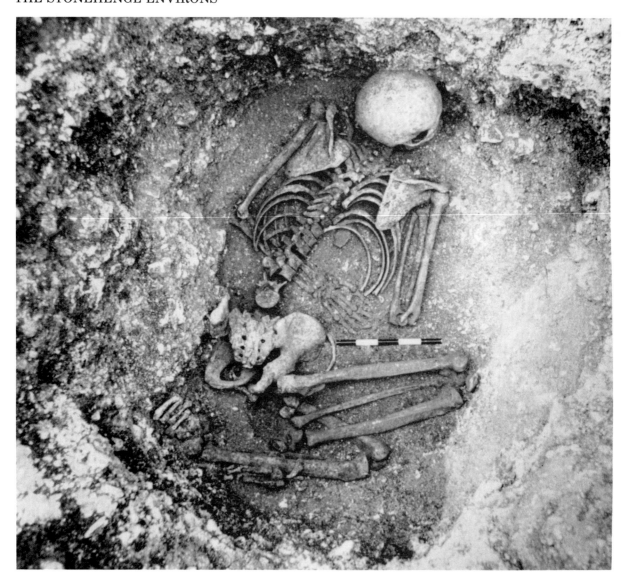

19 *A crouched inhumation burial of the Early Bronze Age recently excavated on Durrington Down.*

to us today. Much remains to be discovered, and answers will no doubt be provided to some of our more fundamental questions, but today's story must rely on today's knowledge. For our understanding of the Stonehenge Environs, this means a reliance on the cumulative wisdom resulting from the energies of several centuries of past students, antiquaries and more recent archaeologists. It is these studies, and the investigators themselves, that will be dealt with in the following chapter.

3

A history of previous enquiries

Occasional finds of Roman pottery at Stonehenge suggest that the monument may have had a curiosity value by the fourth century AD. More certain, is the fact that by 1130 Stonehenge was described in Henry of Huntingdon's *History of England*, and had a name: 'Stanenges'. Minor variations on this name occur in other medieval manuscripts, but all derive partly from 'stan', the Old English word for stone, and either 'hencg', meaning a hinge, or 'hen(c)gen', a gallows. Whichever the correct derivation, it must have referred to the unusual combination of upright stones and lintels.

First illustrated in a fourteenth century manuscript, Stonehenge subsequently became an inevitable subject of antiquarian curiosity. Drawn and engraved in a variety of 'restored' forms, in every conceivable type of landscape, the fruitless speculation as to its architects

20 *William Stukeley's view of Normanton Down engraved in 1723. Allowing for artistic licence, this view is similar to that shown in 4. The mounds shown on the near skyline are those of the Normanton Down Group, with Bush Barrow identified. The enclosure shown running out from the bottom right hand corner of the engraving is the Wilsford Down 'North Kite'.*

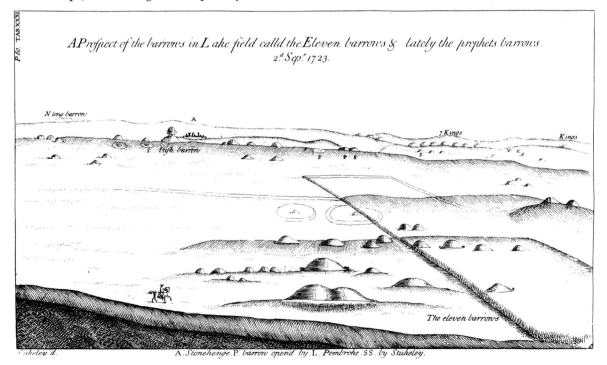

*A Prospect of the barrows in Lake field calld the Eleven barrows & lately the prophets barrows.
2.d Sep.r 1723.*

N long barrow

high barrow

7 Kings

Kings

The eleven barrows

Stukeley d.   A. Stonehenge. P. barrow opend by L. Pembroke. SS. by Stukeley.

A British Druid

21 *Chindonax the British Druid, engraved by William Stukeley in 1724.*

and builders intensified. Alternative candidates included Romans, elements of whose architecture some could clearly discern in the proportions of the stone structures; ninth century Danes or Anglo-Saxons, while the possibility of supernatural intervention was not entirely ruled out. The first move towards investigation rather than mere speculation came in the seventeenth century, when the Wiltshireman John Aubrey, at the command of Charles II, carried out a survey of Stonehenge. On his own admission, his 'review' of 1666 is decidedly sketchy, but his observation was sufficiently acute to notice 'cavities in the ground' which, over 250 years later, were shown by excavation to represent the position of prehistoric pits (the 'Aubrey Holes').

By the beginning of the eighteenth century, shortly after Aubrey's death, it was first accepted that Stonehenge, despite previous attempts at endowing it with a false classical sophistication, was probably a product of the native British population. It was at this time that William Stukeley, a young Lincolnshire doctor, began his topographic tours, carrying on the tradition of observation and investigation started by Aubrey. Stukeley paid his first visit to Stonehenge in 1719, returning annually from 1721 to 1724 in order to survey, measure, draw and occasionally dig. The Stonehenge landscape which Stukeley was able to observe, and which fortunately for future fieldworkers he recorded in a series of drawn 'prospects' (**20**), was very different from that of today. Stukeley walked over 'short grass continually cropt by the flocks of sheep', grass which preserved the marks of ancient earthworks, and his keen observation resulted in remarkable and almost annual discoveries. In August 1721 he discovered the Avenue, two parallel ditches and banks running from the entrance of Stonehenge down into Stonehenge Bottom. In a later year Stukeley was able to follow its course as far as the King Barrow Ridge, where it 'broke off by the plow'd ground', in the open fields of Amesbury where cultivation had levelled the slight earthworks. It was not until over 200 years later that aerial photographs provided the evidence for the remainder of the course of the Avenue, through the 'plow'd ground' as far as the River Avon at West Amesbury.

In 1723, following a second, and less convincing branch of the Avenue, Stukeley came across a 'noble monument of antiquity', a pair of parallel ditches and banks, over 100 m (330 ft) apart, which ran in an east-west direction for a distance of nearly 3km (2 miles). To Stukeley it was clear that this was a hippodrome, a running track for games and races, complete with elevated earthen grandstand at the eastern end. He called it the 'Cursus' (see **64**).

In 1722 and 1723 Stukeley, and Lord Pembroke, dug both within Stonehenge, and, perhaps more profitably, excavated sections through the mounds of some of the surrounding barrows. These sections demonstrated a consistency and care in construction, and the burials he discovered led him to the opinion that the barrows were not constructed for the dead from great battles, but were 'the single

22 *The Lake barrows engraved by Philip Crocker for* Ancient Wiltshire.

sepulchres of kings, and great personages, buried during a considerable space of time, and that in peace'.

Stukeley's fieldwork was, for its period, remarkable, but by the time it was finally published in 1740 both the author and his vision of the past had changed considerably. The title is informative: *The History of the Religion and Temples of the DRUIDS.* Stukeley, who had taken holy orders in 1729, had also become positively obsessive in his enthusiasm for the ancient Druids, elements of whose mystic rites he saw clearly in his ancient temples of Stonehenge and Avebury (**21**). His book, in which subtle differences between his field drawings and the final engraved versions can be detected, does contain the results of his fieldwork in the Stonehenge area, and emphasizes his most important conclusion, that both Stonehenge and the round barrows were of a similar, pre-Roman date. Beyond this, however, the majority of the work is overwhelmingly

Druidic in tone and must be held responsible for the lasting and entirely false association of Druids with Stonehenge.

In the early years of the eighteenth century, in his pre-Druid days, Stukeley was motivated by the excitement of discovery, and found time from his other occupations to indulge his interest. Nearly a century later, it was ill health, and a doctor's prescription to 'ride out or die', that led William Cunnington onto Salisbury Plain and to his interest in its antiquities. By 1801 Cunnington, a wool merchant from the village of Heytesbury on the western edge of Salisbury Plain, had already carried out a number of excavations, including 'digging with a large stick' in the centre of Stonehenge and opening 24 barrows. These excavations were carried out initially under the patronage of H.P. Wyndham, the Member of Parliament for Wiltshire, and later of the Reverend William Coxe, the Rector of Stourton. It was Coxe's intention to write a history of the antiquities of Wiltshire, but in the end this task fell to Sir Richard Colt Hoare, who took over the sponsorship of Cunnington's fieldwork when Coxe's enthusiasm waned. Colt Hoare first met Cunnington 'an ingenious inhabitant and tradesman' in 1801, and shortly afterwards their great collaborative digging campaigns started. Under the overall leadership of Colt Hoare, who provided organization and finance, and who led the searches for new sites to excavate, Cunnington's former digging team remained largely unchanged. Cunnington himself collected the finds and made notes on the discoveries; a father and son team, Stephen and John Parker did the digging; and Philip Crocker, a fine surveyor and draughtsman, produced the maps and plans.

Evidence of the energy of this team can be seen within the Stonehenge Environs, where in the first decade of the nineteenth century over 300 round barrows were excavated. The investigation was usually by means of a single central pit sunk from the summit of the mound, or a trench driven into the centre from the edge of the mound, both appropriate to locating burials which previous experience had shown to be centrally placed. The method now appears crude, the speed of execution, two or three excavations a day (if the mounds were not too large), unimaginable, but more is available for study from these campaigns than from many conducted in the recent past. Records were kept, the barrows numbered and linked to Philip Crocker's extraordinary and accurate perspective plans of the barrow groups (**22**), and many finds were kept and recorded. The burials themselves were considered to be of no great interest. Deposits of cremated bones and entire skeletons were merely noted and returned to the grave, while the pots, jewellery, flint tools, weapons of bronze and iron, and the occasional more spectacular finds (**colour plate 12**) were carried off to the store in Cunnington's Heytesbury garden (**23**).

The fruits of all these investigations, catalogued and illustrated in Colt Hoare's *Ancient Wiltshire* (**24**), and often still available for study in museums (see Appendix - Stonehenge Today), are a testimony to the energy and confidence of Cunnington and Colt Hoare's fieldwork. In the introduction to *Ancient Wiltshire* the latter

pronounces 'We speak from facts not theory', perhaps suggesting that their labours had not brought them any nearer to a greater understanding of the prehistoric past. In truth, the concept of the past had not changed much since Stukeley's days, the main obstacle being the absence of the system, later developed by the Danish antiquary Thomsen, in which prehistory is organized into three successive ages of stone, bronze and iron. Ironically, one of Colt Hoare's circle, the theorist Thomas Leman of Bath, suggested to Cunnington that he could 'distinguish three great eras by the arms of offence found in our barrows', but Cunnington, on the basis of his excavation experience could

23 *The spoils of barrow digging. 'The Antiquary and his daughter carry home the Stonehenge urn May 1802'.*

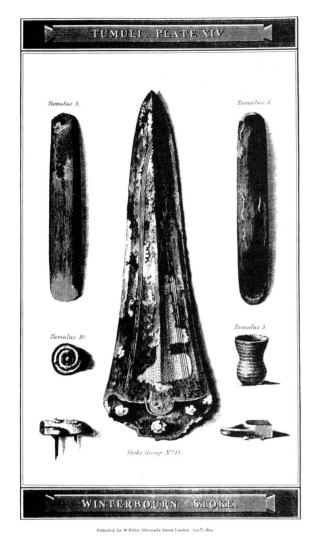

TUMULI. PLATE XIV.

Tumulus 5.

Tumulus 5.

Tumulus 10.

Tumulus 5.

Stoke Group Nº15.

WINTERBOURN STOKE.

Published for W. Miller, Albemarle Street, London, Jany 1 1810.

24 *Engravings of barrow finds from* Ancient Wiltshire. *While accurate and pleasing in appearance, Philip Crocker's finds engravings lack any sense of scale.*

not accept Leman's ideas, and the age of both Stonehenge and the barrows remained incomprehensible.

Cunnington dug three times at Stonehenge, the last of these being in 1810, his final field trip before his death at the end of that year. The lack of exciting finds and the problems of understanding such an enigmatic site probably resulted in his concentration on the more rewarding barrows. The investigation of Stonehenge itself was not to resume until the next century.

Twentieth century investigations

In 1901 it was decided that stone number 56 at Stonehenge, which had been leaning at an ever-increasing angle, should be pulled upright and its base set in concrete. This was carried out under the archaeological supervision of Professor William Gowland who, with remarkable restraint, only excavated an area around the base of the leaning stone sufficient for the engineers to insert the concrete base. His excavation, tightly supervised, the excavated soil sieved (**25**), and meticulously recorded (**26**), shed more light on the construction methods and date of Stonehenge than the preceding centuries of random hole digging and speculation. The evidence from his excavation allowed Gowland to conclude that Stonehenge was built 'during the period of transition from stone to bronze', a date which he estimated at around 1800 BC.

Stonehenge, sold to a private buyer from Wiltshire at auction in 1915, was three years later owned by the nation, which found itself the proud owner of a somewhat unstable monument. Some stones leaned, others were propped up with timber supports, and a restrained programme of restoration was consequently proposed by the Office of Works. For archaeological supervision of its restoration programme, the Office of Works turned to the Society of Antiquaries who, under the guidance of its then president Sir Arthur Evans, expanded the scope of the investigations beyond those necessary for the restoration work. As Professor Gowland was now considered to be too old and frail to undertake the task, the job of archaeological supervisor was entrusted to his intended assistant, Colonel William Hawley.

In the first season, which lasted over a year from November 1919 until December 1920, stone holes were cleared, a start was made on emptying the ditch, the Slaughter Stone was investigated and a number of the rediscovered 'Aubrey Holes' were excavated. This effectively ended the Office of Works' restoration programme, but in 1921 Hawley carried on with his work for the Society of Antiquaries. This programme of work was not finally suspended until 1926, years during which Hawley often worked alone throughout digging seasons, some of which lasted from March until November. Brief annual reports were made which presented the facts but which also demonstrated a growing certainty in Hawley's mind that he would never

25 *Professor Gowland and his team sifting soil at Stonehenge in 1901. Note the Turkish Delight boxes intended for the finds.*

understand Stonehenge. The criticism now levelled at Hawley for his years of patient, unthinking excavation is sometimes considered as unfair, and he was not entirely to blame for the scale of the destruction that was caused for so little gain in knowledge. A full report of Hawley's work might have redeemed him in some eyes, but, with the exception of the annual interim reports, his work was never published and the copious finds were largely dispersed between various museums. Those finds deemed too unexciting to interest any museum were re-interred in a trench at Stonehenge.

Hawley's long seasons of solitary toil had failed to provide any further understanding of Stonehenge's complexities, indeed Hawley's growing confusion is well documented in the series of interim statements. Worse still, the lack of a final report, which could at least have set down the factual side of the excavations, denied the archaeological world any opportunity to make up its own mind about Stonehenge.

It was soon clear that the first priority was to make available the results of Hawley's work, a task taken on in the late 1940s by Professors Richard Atkinson and Stuart Piggott and the Wiltshire archaeologist Dr J.F.S.Stone. Their intention was to produce a definitive excavation report and it was acknowledged from the outset that new excavations would perhaps be necessary to clarify areas of confusion. These initially limited excavations commenced in 1950 with the examination of two of the remaining Aubrey Holes, one of which, hole A32 (see **44**), produced charcoal that was used to give the first absolute date for Stonehenge. Although much quoted, this date is unfortunately so imprecise that it cannot be calibrated and expressed as calendar years BC. As the first radiocarbon date from Stonehenge it has a certain novelty, but beyond this is of little assistance. The programme of research, involving re-excavation of some of Hawley's trenches and limited excavation in previously undisturbed areas, continued for several seasons. As work progressed the remains discovered below ground, particularly those relating to bluestone structures, showed a symmetry which correlated strongly with the fragmentary stone settings visible above ground (27). By 1956 Professor Atkinson felt sufficiently confident to write the book entitled simply *Stonehenge*. In this publication, for the first time, a complex sequence of construction was outlined (see 58) and long-vanished structures of both bluestone and possibly of timber were introduced. Further small areas were excavated by Atkinson and Piggott in 1956 with the intention of refining this sequence, and final stages of investigation relating to the re-erection of specific stones were carried out in 1958 and 1963.

Although the 1963 excavation is the most recent within the stone settings at the centre of Stonehenge, subsequent investigations have added greatly to our understanding of the complete monument. In 1978 John Evans, a

26 *Drawn section through a stone-hole from Gowland's report of 1902.*

leading specialist on the prehistoric environment, re-excavated a 1954 cutting through the Stonehenge ditch and bank. Samples taken in order to analyse land snails, which provide an important key to changes in the environment, revealed an unexpected period of abandonment shortly after the original digging of the ditch. New samples for radiocarbon dating recovered during this excavation pushed the first phase of construction at Stonehenge, back to around 2800 BC, but the most surprising find was a previously unrecognized burial dating to the Beaker period, some time around 2000 BC.

A further surprise came in 1980, when Mike Pitts located the hole for a previously unknown stone in a cable trench running along the roadside verge close to the Heel Stone. The base of this new hole contained the impression of the base of a stone, now preserved in a foam cast (28). This brought to a close the current investigations at Stonehenge itself, with the exception of those routinely carried out whenever there is the necessity to disturb the ground in the vicinity of the monument.

Throughout the twentieth century, when so much attention had been focused on Stonehenge itself, the surrounding landscape had not been entirely neglected. In the early years of the century the southern part of Salisbury Plain became of great importance in the development of military flying, and thus also

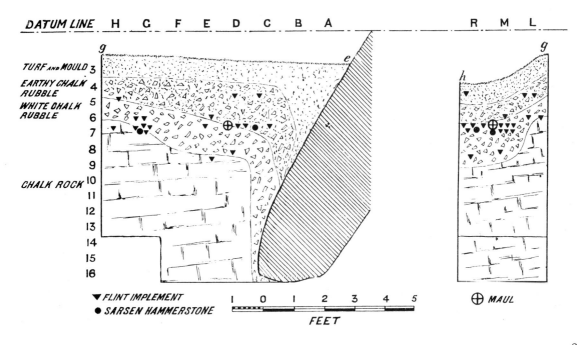

DATUM LINE   H   G   F   E   D   C   B   A   R   M   L

TURF and MOULD 3
EARTHY CHALK 4
RUBBLE 5
WHITE CHALK 5
RUBBLE 6
7
8
9
CHALK ROCK 10
11
12
13
14
15
16

▼ FLINT IMPLEMENT   ⊕ MAUL
● SARSEN HAMMERSTONE

1   0   1   2   3   4   5
FEET

27 *Recent excavations at Stonehenge. The symmetry of the arrangements of stones apparent above ground is reflected in the buried remains.*

of aerial photography. The state of Stonehenge, scarred by trackways and with wooden props holding up the stones, can clearly be seen in a vertical photograph taken from a balloon in 1904 (**29**) and further flying in subsequent decades revealed both new sites and the true form of other examples previously recorded. Woodhenge, the small henge monument close to Durrington Walls, had been thought to be the remains of a large disc barrow flattened by ploughing until an aerial photograph taken in 1925 revealed its true form. The ditch enclosed a series of concentric rings of holes, shown by excavation in 1926-8 to be the remains of timber settings. In later years the Avenue, lost by William Stukeley where it ran into ploughed fields on the King Barrow Ridge, was shown to continue on a curving course which eventually took it down to the River Avon at West Amesbury.

In the course of the twentieth century much of the Stonehenge Environs has seen changes in land-use from downland grass to arable cultivation. These changes, which have allowed through the medium of aerial photography elements of the prehistoric landscape invisible to past observers to be revealed, also pose a considerable threat to the fragile earthen remains of many prehistoric sites. During the 1950s and 1960s the response to the threat from ploughing was to 'rescue' sites by excavation, even those supposedly protected from such damage by legislation. During this period the Stonehenge Environs, like many other areas of the Wessex chalk, saw a considerable number of such excavations, the majority carried out by contract archaeologists working for the then Ministry of Public Buildings and Works. During these decades sites for excavation were apparently selected on an *ad hoc* basis determined largely by the perceived immediacy of the threat. Ploughed examples of both long and round barrows were most commonly examined (**30**), in some cases with unexpected results. The excavation of a supposed pond barrow on Wilsford Down, less than 1.6km (1 mile) south-west of Stonehenge, turned into a major engineering exercise as a cylindrical prehistoric shaft over 30m (100 ft) deep and only 2m (6½ ft) wide was revealed (**31**). The construction of new roads in the area in the 1960s also prompted programmes of salvage excavation and observation work on widely differing scales. Within the henge monument at Durrington Walls major excavations provided a graphic indication of both the scale of construction and of the wealth of interior features (see **77** and **82**). On a much smaller scale, observations close to the Winterbourne Stoke Crossroads barrow cemetery revealed circular post-built huts of Late Bronze Age date (see **102**), the first prehistoric domestic buildings to be discovered in the Stonehenge area.

In 1977 the Secretary of State for the Environment set up a working party to report on the future of Stonehenge and in 1979, to coincide with the anticipated report of this group, the

28 *Rigid polyurethane foam fills the stone-hole discovered next to the Heel Stone in 1980. Despite the evidence of the photograph, the archaeologist surveying the scene does not have his feet embedded in the foam.*

29 *Stonehenge from a balloon 1904.*

Royal Commission on the Historical Monuments of England produced a publication entitled Stonehenge and its Environs. This set out to provide an up-to-date evaluation of the archaeological monuments within the area originally defined by Sir Richard Colt Hoare some 170 years before. Drawing together the results of excavations, aerial photography and ground survey, this publication re-emphasized the true wealth and complexity of the Stonehenge Environs, setting the monuments against a backdrop of land-use both past and present. The survey also clearly demonstrated

30 *'Rescue' excavation of a round barrow near the Lesser Cursus in 1963. A considerable amount of the barrow survived until this time, as shown by the height of the central section left in by the excavators. The ditch of the barrow curves round in the foreground.*

the gaps in our knowledge, noting that 'every monument and topic in the following pages is worthy of further study; in so many instances it has hardly begun'. Recommendations were made, some very specific, suggesting the investigation of an individual site; others more general, noting that the evidence for both settlement and for changes in the past environment was slight.

The Stonehenge Environs Project

To a certain extent the foundations of a continuing research project were laid in the Royal Commission's publication, and many of the themes it emphasized were examined as part of the subsequent Stonehenge Environs Project. Carried out by the Trust for Wessex Archaeology from 1980 onwards, this project set out to investigate some of the fundamental aspects of

prehistoric society which had previously been so neglected. For the first time questions relating to settlement and land-use were to be investigated by means of a systematic programme of fieldwork, survey and excavation. Past excavation had tended towards the examination of a restricted range of prehistoric monument types, resulting inevitably in a bias towards the funerary and ceremonial aspects of the landscape. This was certainly true within the Stonehenge Environs, where the concentration of such monuments, and the absence of traces of domestic activity, had led to the identification of a 'ritual landscape', devoid of everyday life and populated only by the dead. There were hints though, that this was probably not a true picture: as far back as the 1930s pioneering fieldwork had located surface scatters of flint tools thought to represent areas of settlement. This remained an isolated example however, and no subsequent importance was placed on the necessity for enhancing and extending this potential. The location and investigation of settlement traces remained a chance phenomenon, until changes in emphasis in prehistoric research priorities during the 1970s provided the stimulus for investigations

41

31 *Excavation in progress at the Wilsford Shaft in 1960. This excavation turned into a major engineering exercise involving hoists, an air supply and the use of closed-circuit television.*

such as the Stonehenge Environs Project.

As already noted, the Stonehenge Environs, like much of the chalklands of Wessex, are much used for arable cultivation. In the recent past the effects of cultivation, particularly on upstanding earthwork monuments has inevitably been detrimental (**32**). However unfortunate its effects, such land-use does provide extensive opportunities for fieldwork involving surface collection, more generally known as 'fieldwalking'. This method of survey involves the careful and systematic collection of artefacts from the surface of cultivated fields, ideally after a period of frost and rain which washes clean the surface finds and makes them easier to recognize. As may be expected, there

is an inevitable bias towards those more robust objects, such as tools of flint and stone, which will survive both the processes of mechanical cultivation and also the effects of winter frosts.

Flint for tools and weapons was of vital importance up to the Neolithic period, and continued to be significant even after the introduction of metal. Flint occurs in a variety of forms, as round nodules or thin seams within chalk, or as boulders or pebbles within deposits of gravel or clay. In many areas it occurs close to or on the surface, where nodules may be flawed by the action of frost, necessitating some excavation to obtain sound raw material. In the Stonehenge area there is no shortage of flint, much of mediocre quality, and the surfaces of ploughed fields are carpeted with broken pieces of flint amongst which lie flint tools and the waste material of flint working. The identification of humanly-worked pieces from within such an overwhelming background 'noise' requires skill and an understanding of the principles of flint working.

As flint is almost pure silica, it has some of the same characteristics as glass, no internal 'grain' and a consistent way of fracturing. When it is hit correctly flint breaks with a 'conchoidal' (shell-like) fracture, concentric rings spreading like ripples out from the point of impact (**33**). For any impact to remove a piece, known as a 'flake' from its parent block (the 'core'), the angle of percussion needs to be less than 90 degrees (point F). This angle is the one between the surface of the core where the impact is to fall (the 'platform') and the edge of the core. Any more than 90 degrees (point N) and the impact, no matter how strong, will be unsuccessful and will only internally fracture the core. As well as the conchoidal rings already mentioned, each flake exhibits other individual characteristics: part of the platform of the core from which it was removed, and traces of a cone-shaped peak at the actual point of impact, the 'point of percussion'. The core will naturally retain the concave impression of the same characteristics until the next flake is removed. These are known as 'flake scars'. It is these characteristics, both complete and in a fragmentary form, which must be recognized by those involved in fieldwalking and the excavation of prehistoric sites.

Employing the principles of flint working ('knapping') outlined above (**34**), flakes can be removed from a core to provide sharp-edged

32 *The barrows of the unusual Lake Down Group lie isolated within an area of arable cultivation. This small group contains a high proportion of rare pond barrows and may therefore fall late in the overall sequence of barrow group construction.*

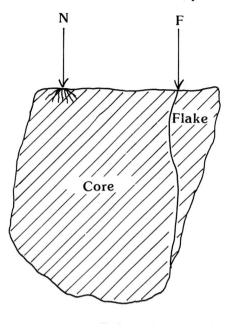

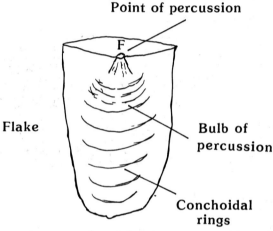

33 *The principles of flint knapping. A blow of point F will remove a flake; a blow at N will always fail.*

tools which, without any further modification, are entirely suitable for a number of cutting tasks. Such flakes can be modified by the removal of subsequent smaller flakes to form tools more suitable for specific functions, such as scrapers with a more chisel-like edge for the removal of fat from hides (**35**); or awls for boring holes in wood or leather (see **96**). Alternatively, heavier tools such as axes can be produced from a block of flint by the removal of flakes (see **85**). Such 'core tools' are usually shaped by alternately flaking one side and then the other ('bifacial working').

As a first and vital stage of the Environs project over 700 ha (1700 acres) of cultivated fields surrounding Stonehenge were examined, and a sample of the surface artefacts collected for analysis. These were predominantly worked flints, both tools and the waste products of flint quarrying and tool production. Some areas, particularly those which had only been in cultivation for the past few decades also produced pottery of Neolithic and Bronze Age date. From this, the first stage of investigation, a number of broad zones as well as more restricted scatters could be identified. In specific cases, and generally only as a prelude to excavation, a more detailed stage of surface collection and associated survey was carried out. This detailed approach, which inevitably concentrated on smaller areas, involved not only the collection, within a rigidly defined grid, of a larger sample of surface artefacts, but also the examination of the chemical and magnetic properties of the soil in which they lay. In a very small number of cases the final stage of this process involved the excavation of areas of plough-soil to retrieve the complete assemblage of artefacts and to examine the underlying chalk for more positive traces of activity in the form of pits or post-holes. Such traces were located in several instances (**36**) where undisturbed deposits, protected from the effects of ploughing in small pits, provided the more fragile remains of pottery, animal bone, charcoal and seeds.

This aspect of the project was intended to answer the question of whether or not the area around Stonehenge was populated during the time that Stonehenge itself was being built and used. The visual evidence provided by the many burial mounds and other sites related to ceremony had tended to suggest an entirely ritual landscape, but only a systematic search for the slighter traces of more everyday activities would confirm whether or not this was the case. Other questions were concerned with the date and function of specific monuments, and with overall changes in the prehistoric environment. Many of these could only be answered by excavation and consequently, over the four seasons of fieldwork, a total of 15 excavations were carried out. These ranged greatly in scale, from the first excavation carried out by the project, the extensive sample of Coneybury Henge in 1980, to tiny trenches dug in order to examine the soil sequence in the dry valley

34 *A prehistoric flint knapper (Jane Brayne).*

35 *Hide preparation using a flint scraper. The chisel-like edge, prepared by 'retouching' a sharp flake edge will remove fat without cutting the hide (Jane Brayne).*

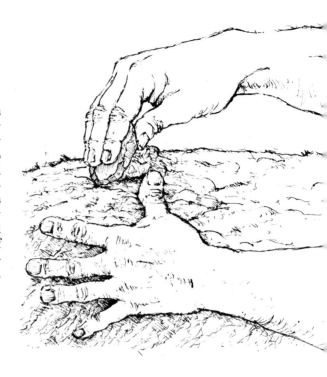

bottoms surrounding Stonehenge.

On all of the more substantial excavations geophysical survey was carried out, primarily with a magnetometer capable of accurately locating the position of ditches or pits cut into the underlying chalk (**37**). Such survey enabled sample trenches to be positioned with exceptional accuracy. Before any plough-soil was removed it was routinely and systematically sampled for traces of enhanced magnetism and phosphates, potential indicators of areas of burning and of human or animal waste respectively. Only then was the plough-soil excavated,

36 *Excavation on the King Barrow Ridge 1983. The removal of the thin top-soil revealed Neolithic pits, the filling of which was extensively sieved in order to recover small finds, animal bones and seeds.*

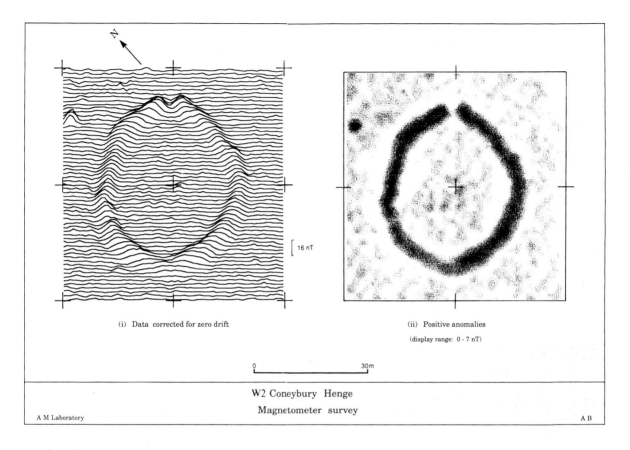

N

16 nT

(i) Data corrected for zero drift

(ii) Positive anomalies

(display range: 0 - 7 nT)

0   30m

W2 Coneybury Henge

Magnetometer survey

A M Laboratory

A B

37 *Geophysical survey plot of Coneybury Henge. Both types of display show the shape of the enclosure ditch and the position of the entrance. The pale irregular band on the dot matrix plot (on the right) even indicates the position of the long vanished bank.*

by hand, within a rigidly-defined 3 ft (c. 1m) grid, a departure from the practices of earlier decades when the majority of such deposits were removed by machine down to the surface of the chalk. Any artefacts from the plough-soil are clearly of some considerable significance and in order to standardize their retrieval 25 per cent of the soil was routinely sieved. The sieve swinging on a scaffold frame was a familiar site on all the excavations carried out as part of the Stonehenge Environs Project and provided samples of the full range of artefacts

contained within the modern plough-soil as well as backache. The approach of the excavations of the 1980s was to regard the hitherto neglected plough-soils overlying the chalk as an integral part of the record of the site, and to excavate them with care. It was vindicated in a few cases by the correlation of areas of enhanced magnetism and phosphates with scatters of flint tools and pottery, providing the clues to prehistoric activities irrecoverable by other, more conventional methods.

In its entirety the Stonehenge Environs Project generated a huge quantity of artefacts and a considerable body of data for environmental and dating studies. The cataloguing and analysis of this material, the 'post-excavation' stage, is now complete, and a summary of the results published in the form of a monograph, which it is hoped will act as the stimulus to further work in the Stonehenge Environs.

4

Stonehenge: the evidence

The past few decades have seen a great outpouring of writing related to Stonehenge, a great variety of books, papers, pamphlets and articles written with varying degrees of authority and reliability. At times it is difficult to separate the facts from the fiction, the evidence from unfounded speculation. Imagination should not be banished entirely when attempting to reconstruct Stonehenge, or indeed any aspect of the prehistoric past, but the very personal, subjective vision which is often produced by imagination should always be acknowledged as such.

The display boards at Stonehenge confront us with questions even before we pass through the turnstiles (38). Turning to hard facts, which even Professor Atkinson, the one person who should know, admitted as being few and far between, the evidence from archaeological investigation and analysis can provide at least partial answers to some of the questions posed about Stonehenge. We know where it is, we know (with reservations) what it is and we can be certain about its general age, if not the of the finer details of its internal chronology. Answers to the question of how it was built must rely on practicality, experiment and a measure of inspired guesswork, while serious attempts at answering the question of why Stonehenge was built and for what purpose, depend on attempts at understanding the prehistoric mind, a mind with fears and aspirations far removed from our own.

The physical setting of Stonehenge has already been described and although essentially undistinguished, has a certain presence within the landscape, difficult to appreciate when speeding past on the A303 or dodging the sightseers crossing the A344. The question of

the exact siting of Stonehenge is often raised: why was this particular spot chosen for the construction of the original earthwork enclosure? It was certainly not for prominence, as any of the surrounding low ridges, many of which were later enhanced by the addition of

38 *'Who built Stonehenge?' a question for the visitor.*

clusters of round barrows, would have served better. But in any case the first monument, unless it contained a substantial timber structure, may well have been visually quite unimpressive, and even if sited on a hill top would not have been very visible from a distance. In short the answer to the question of why Stonehenge is sited where it is, is that we do not know.

What is Stonehenge?

In archaeological terminology Stonehenge is classified as a henge, or henge monument, one of the loose group of Late Neolithic monuments which range in scale from tiny circles of deep pits to massive earthwork enclosures the size of Avebury or Durrington Walls (see **77**). It is clear from those that have been investigated

that, although broadly similar in date, no similar consistency of function can be discerned. Some contain traces of timber buildings and may have functioned as settlements. Others, in contrast, contain large collections of highly-decorated pottery and other 'exotic' items, deposited in a very structured manner, suggesting a more ceremonial function. Within this class of monument, to which part of its name has been given, Stonehenge remains something of an anomaly. Its overall shape conforms to the general pattern: many henges are circular or slightly oval. The majority, however, have an external bank whereas the main bank at Stonehenge is internal, and outside the ditch

39 *Overall plan of Stonehenge.*

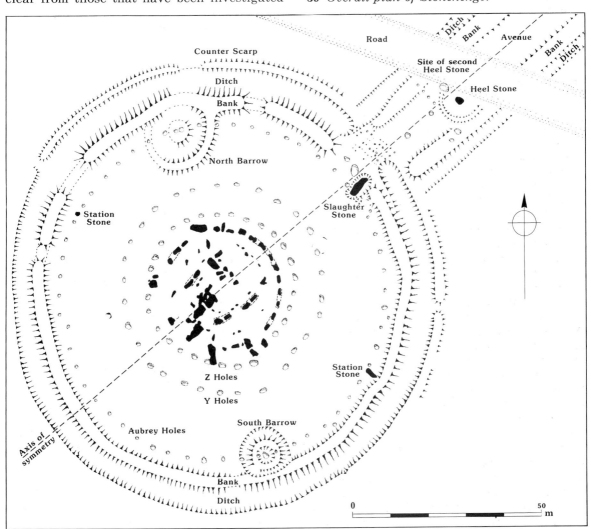

40 *The Heel Stone.*

there is only a slight 'counterscarp' bank. Many henges contain symmetrical settings of timber or, in areas where suitable stone is readily available, settings of stones. But no other henge incorporates stones which have apparently been moved over the considerable distances indicated by those at Stonehenge. Finally, despite the use of stone in other henges, no other example exhibits such refinements of design as shaped and jointed stones, or horizontal lintels placed on top of uprights. In addition to this series of unique attributes Stonehenge exhibits a long history of construction, use and modification which cannot be identified at any similar site. Stonehenge is far from typical and is a highly inappropriate type site.

Physically Stonehenge is a ruined building set within an earthwork enclosure; only the robustness of the majority of the stone employed in its construction having ensured its partial survival into the twentieth century. In addition to this, the very isolation of the site during the medieval period and beyond must have helped to protect it from the attentions of stone breakers, those whose efforts so decimated the stone settings of Avebury in the seventeenth and eighteenth centuries. If Stonehenge had sat within a medieval village, rather than in relative isolation within the little used areas of sheep pasture, beyond the extent even of the cultivated fields, then that village would now almost certainly possess some fine cobbled pavements and sturdy walls at the expense of the prehistoric stones.

The structure of Stonehenge

Leaving aside for a moment the Avenue, which links Stonehenge into a much wider landscape, it is simplest to introduce the various elements that make up Stonehenge starting from the outside and working inwards. This, for the present purposes, deliberately sets aside the time dimension, to be discussed below. We know that construction and modification went on over a period perhaps as long as 1500 years, but sequence and dating will be considered only after the overall structure of Stonehenge is appreciated.

Some of the elements that make up the whole monument are very obvious. The stone settings for example, are visible, and their basic layout

can be appreciated even in their ruined state. Others, such as pits and post-holes dug into the underlying chalk, are now invisible at ground level and their position is known only from excavation (**39**).

The Heel Stone

The outermost element is the Heel Stone (**40**) a large upright unworked sarsen which lies immediately adjacent to the old turnpike road from Amesbury to Shrewton, now the busy A344. Sarsen, a type of hard sandstone, is found only in the form of occasional small rounded boulders in the vicinity of Stonehenge. The nearest source of large sarsens, of the size represented by the Heel Stone and the other sarsens at Stonehenge is on the Marlborough Downs about 30km (18 miles) to the north-east.

41 *The possible route of the sarsens from the Marlborough Downs.*

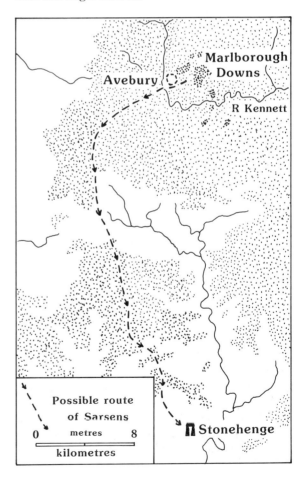

Here, close to the Avebury henge, although many areas have been cleared of these stones which formed such an obstruction to cultivation, in some coombes and valley bottoms huge sarsens can still be seen lying in their original positions. There is effectively only one potential route overland from the Marlborough Downs to Stonehenge (41), involving some steep slopes and valley bottoms which may have still been well-wooded and presented a considerable obstacle to progress. It can only be assumed that the sarsens were transported on some type of sledge, possibly assisted by rollers when the terrain allowed, with the motive force provided by a combination of human and animal power. As yet no one has attempted to replicate the transport of a suitable-sized sarsen in order to test these suggestions.

Although the Heel Stone now appears in isolation, it may originally have had a twin, the stone which stood in the hole recorded by Mike Pitts in 1980. No trace of this can now be seen in the roadside verge of the A344. The Heel Stone is now the only stone still standing outside the earthwork enclosure, but excavation has revealed the holes for two additional stones, lying along the 'axis of symmetry', a hypothetical line running through the entrance of the earthwork enclosure. In addition a line

of four holes, apparently for timber uprights, has been located close to the Heel Stone.

The earthwork enclosure

Moving inwards from the Heel Stone, the earthwork enclosure is the next element of Stonehenge to be encountered. This consists of a ditch which, where lengths have been examined by excavation, has been shown to be extremely irregular, both in width and in depth, reminiscent of the 'string of sausages' appearance of some causewayed enclosure ditches. The depth of the ditch where excavated by Colonel Hawley varied between 1.5 m (4½ ft) and 2 m (7 ft). The chalk excavated from this ditch appears to have been used to construct both the interior bank, the height of which was calculated by Professor Atkinson as being about 1.8 m (6 ft) and the much shallower external counterscarp bank. It is uncertain whether the original appearance of the bank mirrored the irregularity of the ditch profile and also if the bank incorporated any structure, or was simply an unsupported dump of chalk.

42 *The Slaughter Stone, originally upright, its rusty, stained hollows giving rise to lurid and unfounded tales of sacrifice.*

43 *The Station stone on the south-eastern side of Stonehenge with the Heel Stone in the background.*

It is known that there were at least two original entrances, the one now visible (facing north-east) and one to the south. Excavation has demonstrated that the current entrance to the earthwork enclosure is a modification of the original. Some time after the construction of the enclosure the alignment of the entrance was shifted slightly by digging away part of the original chalk causeway and backfilling a corresponding 8 m (26 ft) length of the ditch to the south-east. The reasons for such mod-ification will be discussed below.

The Slaughter Stone

Lying within the entrance is an unworked and now recumbent sarsen stone, its surface covered with shallow depressions, stained a rusty red. This is the 'Slaughter Stone' (**42** and **colour plate 1**), its name the product of a past imagination which saw the rusty depressions as receptacles for sacrificial blood. More mun-danely, the staining is caused by rainwater acting on iron within the stone and the sacrifi-cial function would have been made more difficult by the fact that the Slaughter Stone

originally stood upright. The holes for two further stones have been located within the entrance of the enclosure, together with a line of post-holes.

The Station Stones

Arranged around the inner edge of the earth-work bank were originally four small upright sarsens, the 'Station Stones', of which two can still be seen. Number 93 is shaped and still stands upright (**43**), the other, the unworked number 91 has fallen although its stone-hole can clearly be seen. Two were originally sur-rounded by shallow circular ditches with exter-nal banks, of which the most prominent is the 'south barrow'.

The Aubrey Holes

Lying immediately adjacent to the bank within the earthwork enclosure is a ring of 56 pits, known as the 'Aubrey Holes', the position of excavated examples marked by circular con-crete spots in both the grass and on the path. Their original discoverer, the seventeenth cen-tury antiquary John Aubrey, noted regularly spaced depressions in the turf, but they were not confirmed as pits until Hawley's excavations. Both Hawley's, and later Atkinson's investi-gations suggested that these pits had never

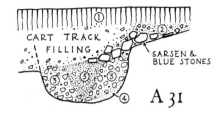

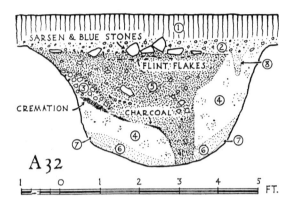

44 *Drawn sections of Aubrey Holes 31 and 32 from Atkinson, Piggott and Stone's 1952 report.*

held upright timbers or stones, and in many cases they produced evidence in their upper levels for the burial of small quantities of cremated human bone (**44**).

The 'Y' and 'Z' Holes

Although part of the area between the inner edge of the bank and the outermost stone settings was extensively excavated by Hawley, it is still far from certain what might lie within this zone of the monument. Records of Hawley's work are sparse, and references to 'trenching' may suggest that areas were examined in a series of strips, possibly quite narrow, and within which certain types of information may not easily have been recognized. What is certain though, is that this zone includes at least two further settings of pits, the 'Y' and 'Z' holes. These run concentric with the outermost element of the central stone structure and, although they are suggested as having been dug in order to hold upright stones, possibly surplus bluestones, they appear never to have done so.

The central stone settings

There now remains the stone settings, the massive and sophisticated arrangements that set Stonehenge apart from any other prehistoric monument in western Europe. Two types of stone are used in their construction: sarsen, already mentioned in the context of the Heel Stone, the Slaughter Stone and the Station Stones, and bluestone. The sarsens used in the central settings, despite being from the same general source as the above, are much larger, weighing up to 45 tonnes, representing both more deliberate choice and a greater degree of committment in their transportation. We can only assume that once selected for size, the sarsens were perhaps roughly shaped where they lay, if only to check for flaws and more practically to remove any excess weight before their transportation. Prehistoric henge builders should not be assumed to be devoid of common sense, even if their constructions often seem inexplicable.

The bluestones

Bluestone is a misleading term as it encompasses a number of differing rock types, united by a common source, a restricted area within the Preseli Mountains in south-west Wales. Identified types within this broad group include rhyolite, spotted dolerite, volcanic ash, Cosheston sandstone and calcareous ash, none of which are strictly blue. Rhyolite, when worn

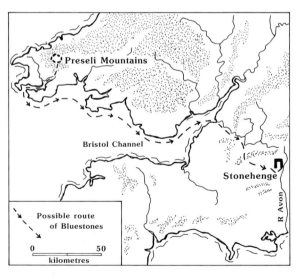

45 *The possible route of the bluestones from the Preseli Mountains.*

smooth and particularly when wet, can take on a blue-grey appearance, while the most striking of the bluestones is the greeny-blue dolerite, its surface peppered with small white spots. The most widely accepted theory concerning the bluestones is to regard their arrival on Salisbury Plain as the result of human effort, with the most likely route being partly overland and partly by water (**45**). The final stage of the journey traditionally involves a trip along the River Avon (**colour plate 10**).

No trace of the routes suggested for either the sarsens or the bluestones has yet been found, although over the past few years there have been several unsubstantiated reports of 'bluestones' being found by divers in rivers close to their supposed route from Wales. Such an occurrence, if it ever were to become a reality, would have the potential to answer questions beyond those relating simply to the route of the stones (see below). Wales is certainly a long distance to transport stones weighing up to 4 tonnes. Professor Atkinson did demonstrate, however, that stones the size of the bluestones could be dragged on a sledge by a party of 32 schoolboys, whose numbers could be reduced to 14 by the introduction of wooden rollers. When water-borne on a composite boat, the same stone could be man- ouevred quite easily by 4 schoolboys, an exercise compared by Professor Atkinson with the 'pleasant pastime' of punting.

Despite the general acceptance of the idea of human transport for the bluestones, alternative suggestions, originally proposed some time ago but generally dismissed, have recently been revived. New research by Dr Williams-Thorpe of the Open University claims to show clear proof that the action of glaciers was responsible for the transportation of the bluestones to Wiltshire where they were located as a patch of 'erratics'. Much of the evidence for the case for glacial transport appears however, to be circumstantial, with perhaps the strongest counter-argument being provided by the total absence within Wessex of large bluestones other than those incorporated within prehistoric monuments. Small chips of bluestone are occasionally found on the surface of fields surrounding Stonehenge, but the prehistoric builders are unlikely to have discovered *and* used the entire stock of available glacial erratics. Human transport, despite the distances and effort required, still seems a more reasonable concept.

There are further areas of uncertainty concerning the bluestones. The full description below of their final arrangement at Stonehenge contains a suggestion that they may previously have stood, though not necessarily at Stonehenge, in an arrangement which included

46 *Stonehenge: the stone settings today.*

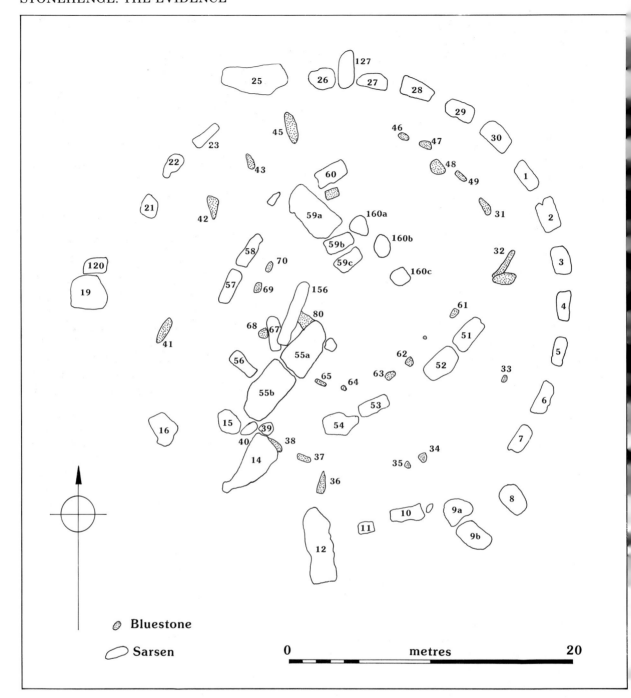

47 *Stonehenge: detailed plan of the stone settings.*

trilithons. There is the possibility that the bluestones were not transported from Wales as rough blocks of stone, to be shaped once they arrived on Salisbury Plain. They may have stood instead as a circle or other arrangement of shaped stones in Wales, an arrangement which may have included the novel idea of uprights and horizontal lintels in stone. It is perhaps an entire stone circle which was

48 *Stonehenge: the stone settings viewed from the air. Even in such a ruined state elements of symmetry can be appreciated. The most striking elements are the subtly curved outer sarsen circle and the individual trilithons which make up the inner sarsen horseshoe (Mick Aston).*

to Salisbury Plain, the most crucial question to be asked will be whether or not it is shaped. If it is, then the idea presented above may be nearer the truth than can currently be asserted.

Viewed from ground level, and particularly now unrestricted access is no longer possible, the central stones may not at first seem to form

uprooted and brought to Stonehenge, a suggestion which, if accepted, may help to explain the variety of stones within the all-encompassing term 'bluestone'. We cannot even guess at the significance with which such 'foreign' stones might have been endowed, but if it were only stones that were being brought from Preseli, logic might suggest that one type, durable and contrasting with the locally-available sarsens, might have been selected. Spotted dolerite would be a strong candidate for this. However, if stones had already been selected, shaped and imbued with a significance beyond their use as simple building blocks by their incorporation within a symbolic structure, then choice would have been constrained. Perhaps we should see the bluestones as a 'job lot'. If a 'bluestone' is ever found along the supposed route from Wales

49 *The method of jointing stones in the outer sarsen circle (Linda Coleman).*

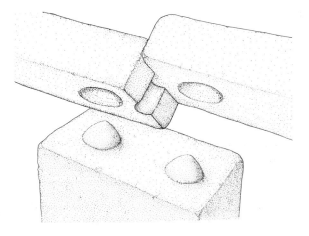

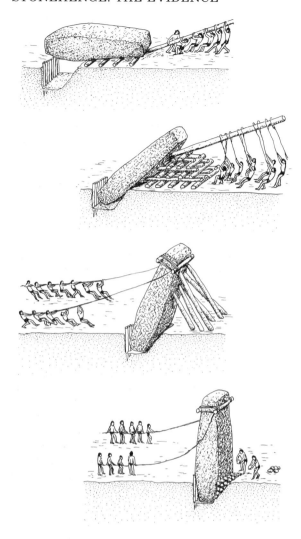

50 *The method of raising upright stones in ramped stone-holes.*

any particularly coherent pattern (**46**). When viewed in plan however (**47**), even the fragmentary ruins take on a coherence which can be summarized very simply.

The sarsen circle

In its complete form the outermost stone setting consisted of a circle of 30 upright sarsens, of which 17 still stand, each weighing about 25 tonnes. The tops of these uprights were linked by a continuous ring of horizontal sarsen lintels, only a small part of which is now still in position (**48** and **colour plate 7**) . The contrast

with the unworked sarsen Heel Stone and Slaughter Stone could not be greater. Those in the sarsen circle are carefully shaped, their surfaces and edges are dressed smooth and the individual stones jointed together. The horizontal lintels are not only firmly fixed onto the uprights by means of simple mortice-and-tenon joints, consisting of projections and corresponding hollows, but are also locked to each other end to end using what is effectively a tongue-and-groove joint (**49**). The shaping and jointing, seen again in the central sarsen settings, shows the application of building techniques more appropriate to wood, but here carried out in unyielding stone. Close observation reveals yet more sophistication in the outer sarsen circle, as the edges of the horizontal lintels are smoothed into a gentle curve, a curve which follows the line of the entire circle. Such sophistication, seen also in the gently-tapering upright sarsen pillars, raises Stonehenge far above the simple selection and raising of unhewn stones seen at many other stone circles, many of which should more correctly be referred to as stone rings, within the British Isles.

Excavation has provided considerable detail of the methods employed in both shaping stone and in erecting the upright pillars. All excavations at Stonehenge have produced great quantities of sarsen 'mauls', round battered stones ranging from a cricket ball to a football in size. These were used to batter the surface of the sarsens and bluestones to shape with a combination of flaking edges (in the same way that flint is worked) and 'pecking' flat surfaces. The complexity of the joints in the sarsen structures appear even more of an achievement when it is realized that the stone removed in their creation was removed a few small chips and grains at a time.

In order to erect the upright stones ramped stone-holes were prepared, the base of the stone slid over the ramped edge, then hauled upright and packed in place with stone fragments, chalk and earth (**50**). It is assumed that the stones were hauled into their upright position by human effort, possibly assisted by draught animals. Substantial ropes must have been needed, perhaps of twisted vegetable fibre, thickened versions of the cord found in the waterlogged fill of the Wilsford Shaft. Alternatively thongs of plaited hide may have been used to take the weight of the huge uprights.

51 *Raising a sarsen lintel on a timber 'crib'.*

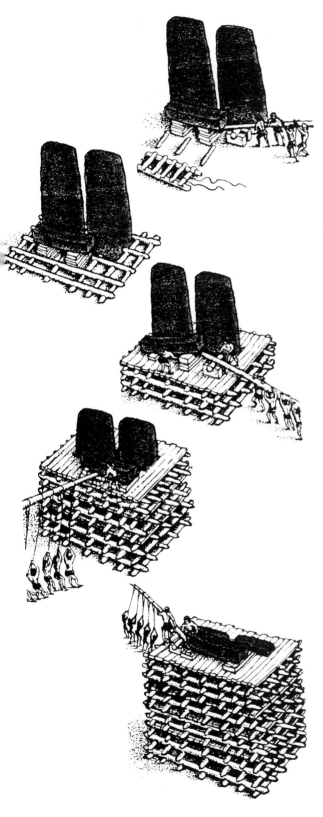

This still leaves the often-asked question of how the horizontal lintels were raised onto the uprights. There are two methods by which this is suggested as having been achieved. The first involves the construction of a timber 'crib', a platform of horizontally-laid timbers on which the stone was placed at ground level and gradually raised up a little at a time (**51**), by levering up one end and inserting another timber before repeating the process at the other end. Once raised to the height of the uprights on which it was to be placed the lintel would then be slid sideways and lowered onto them, its mortice holes located precisely over the top of the projecting tenons of the uprights. The other suggestion involves the construction of great sloping ramps of chalk rubble and earth up which the lintels were dragged before being dropped into place. Whichever method, or an alternative not yet suggested, was employed, some considerable care would have had to be exercised in the working of the mortices and their corresponding tenons in order to ensure a tight fit. This may have involved the final working of the mortice holes being carried out immediately before they were placed over the tenons, at the time that the lintel was already raised to its full height. Alternatively, the final packing of the uprights could have been left to this stage in order to provide the means for slight adjustments in their angle and thus facilitate the final jointing. Some of the post-holes recovered by excavation in the centre of Stonehenge have been suggested as the remains of wooden scaffolding, possibly the remains of the sort of timber platforms described above. The construction, and subsequent removal, of earth ramps would leave no trace for archaeologists to recover.

Within, and concentric to, the outer sarsen circle is a circular setting of upright bluestones, originally about 60 in number (**colour plate 8**). Some have fallen or been crushed by falling sarsens, others of a soft volcanic ash have actually dissolved above ground level and their position can only be seen when excavation reveals the surviving stumps. Some bluestones in this circle exhibit unusual features, out of keeping with this, their final arrangement, and suggesting that they had previously been arranged in a radically different manner. The

original use of stone 150, now a fallen upright, was obviously as a horizontal lintel. Of the two mortice holes, one is still quite clearly visible (**52**), the other half buried in the grass. None of the other bluestones retain complete corresponding tenons, although these would have been relatively easy to remove once redundant, unlike the deeply worked mortice holes. However, recognizable traces of tenons survive on stones 67, 69 and 70 and appear to result from such modification.

Inside these two circles lie two further concentric stone settings, both broadly of a horseshoe shape, and again one each of sarsen and bluestone.

The sarsen horseshoe
The outermost horseshoe originally consisted of five sarsen trilithons, (trilithon = Greek *tri-lithos*, three stones), each comprising two uprights and a horizontal lintel (**53**). The scale of each of these individual stone arrangements is huge, the tallest stones, which weigh over 45 tonnes, supporting massive lintels at a height of over 7 m (22 ft) above ground level. Although now fragmentary, enough survives of this arrangement to show the careful height grading of the five trilithons, ranging from the lowest pair, those flanking the open side of the horseshoe, to the tallest, the Great Trilithon, now ruinous after one upright and the massive lintel fell in 1797 (**colour plate 9**). The base of the shattered fallen upright, with a huge 'heel' left on presumably to assist stability, shows the shallow depth to which it was buried. The necessity for the extra height may have contributed to its eventual fall, although it had stood unaided for nearly 4000 years.

The careful selection and subsequent shaping evident in the sarsens of the outer circle is again demonstrated in the sarsen trilithon horseshoe. Lintels are locked onto their uprights by means of mortice-and-tenon joints, and the uprights are gently tapered from the base upwards. This tapering, which has the effect of increasing the apparent height of the stones, is clearly deliberate. Given the sophistication apparent

52 *Mortice holes in a fallen bluestone showing clear evidence of its former use as a lintel. Only one can be seen, in deep shadow half obscured by a leaning bluestone. The other lies buried in the grass where the sunlight strikes the stone.*

in other constructional details, the creation of an optical illusion should perhaps be regarded as more likely than the alternative, that the builders were imitating the natural tapering form of a tree trunk.

It was on the surface of one of the uprights of the sarsen horseshoe that carvings were first noted in 1953. Not the graffiti that demonstrates the long-standing popularity of Stonehenge as a tourist attraction, but shallower, more subtle carvings of prehistoric axes and a dagger (**54** and see **107**). The axes are of a flat, earlier Bronze Age form, but the dagger appears to be of a more exotic form, best paralleled in the royal graves of Mycenae. To some this provided clear proof of the hand of a Mycenaean builder at Stonehenge, a concept that was not completely discounted until more widely available radiocarbon dates proved it to be chronologically impossible.

Enfolded within this massive protective horseshoe, lies a smaller horseshoe arrangement of upright bluestones, some finely shaped, their sides worked into vertical grooves and projections reminiscent of the tongue-and-groove joints of the sarsen circle lintels (**55**). This may indicate the creation of 'composite' stones, to be used in circumstances where a large stone was required but was unavailable. Finally, within this bluestone horseshoe lies the Altar Stone, a dressed block of blue-grey sandstone from the shores of Milford Haven in Pembrokeshire. Astride the axis of symmetry and now partly buried by the ruins of the Great Trilithon, the Altar Stone probably stood upright as a pillar at the focal point of the entire monument.

Lost elements
These circles, horseshoes, pits, post- and stone-holes, are the more certain elements that can either be seen or can be deduced from the available records of past excavations. Even these make up a monument of considerable complexity and yet it is certain that they do not represent the complete picture. The sequence of construction originally presented by Professor Atkinson (and discussed below) includes two additional arrangements of bluestones, both subsequently removed and their component stones rearranged. The first of these, suggested as having been erected prior to any of the sarsen structures, is a double circle of bluestones, abandoned prior to

53 *In the foreground lie the shattered remains of a sarsen trilithon, beyond which smaller stones of the bluestone horseshoe can be seen in front of a surviving sarsen trilithon. The stone on the far left of the picture is the fallen lintel of the great trilithon, in which one of the mortice holes can clearly be seen.*

completion. The chalk-cut pits, in the base of which the impressions of stones could be seen, were called by their excavator the 'dumb-bells'. A number of examples were located, but objectively the plan cannot be used to support the regular and extensive arrangement suggested by Professor Atkinson. Within this arrangement some emphasis on the axis of symmetry can clearly be seen, and also on this line Colonel Hawley discovered one of the few burials to be located at Stonehenge. Despite considerable disturbance to the grave, with the consequence that no firm indication of its date could be obtained, its position strongly suggests that it is contemporary with the main stone structures.

The second proposed bluestone arrangement is an oval setting within the sarsen horseshoe, the components of which were shortly afterwards rearranged into the bluestone structures visible today. These arrangements may have existed, although on the basis of available excavation information, a number of alternatives can be suggested.

All of the excavations at Stonehenge have revealed post-holes, presumed to have originally held timber uprights. Many examples have been found within the area of the stone settings, and in the zone between the stones and the bank, where regular lines have been recognized. The purpose of all these holes remains uncertain, as the methods of excavation previously employed would not allow patterns to be easily identified. Those within the stone settings may be interpreted as the base of poles for scaffolding or, more imaginatively, as Professor Atkinson has speculated, as traces of a 'possible, or even probable' timber building.

54 *The prehistoric carvings on stone 53.*

55 *A vertically-grooved bluestone behind which is the massive fallen lintel of the great trilithon.*

The inhumation located by Hawley was not the only one to be found at Stonehenge as in 1978 investigations carried out by John Evans, exploring the environmental potential, located a grave cut into the upper silts of the ditch. The burial was that of a Beaker age man who died in about 2100 BC, an archer to judge from the stone wrist-guard found with his skeleton (see **17** and **56**). Barbed-and-tanged flint arrowheads found with his body might also be taken as an indication of his role in life, but for the fact that the tips of two of them were found embedded in his bones and were almost certainly the cause of his death.

It has already been noted that parts of Stonehenge remain unexplored or incompletely investigated, and although it is unlikely that major new elements remain undiscovered, the potential for as yet unconfirmed phases of construction must not be dismissed.

The Avenue

The Stonehenge Avenue has so far only been briefly mentioned, an omission which must be rectified as it is an integral part of the complete monument of Stonehenge. It consists of twin banks about 12 m (40 ft) apart with internal ditches, and begins at the remodelled entrance to the earthwork enclosure. From here the first section runs straight down the gentle slope for a distance of about 530 m (560 yds) into Stonehenge Bottom (**57**). Between the entrance to the enclosure and the Heel Stone Colonel Hawley found the holes for two stones, and geophysical survey along this first section has provided hints of other stone-holes. The Heel Stone may originally not have stood in such

56 *The burial of the archer in the Stonehenge ditch (Jane Brayne).*

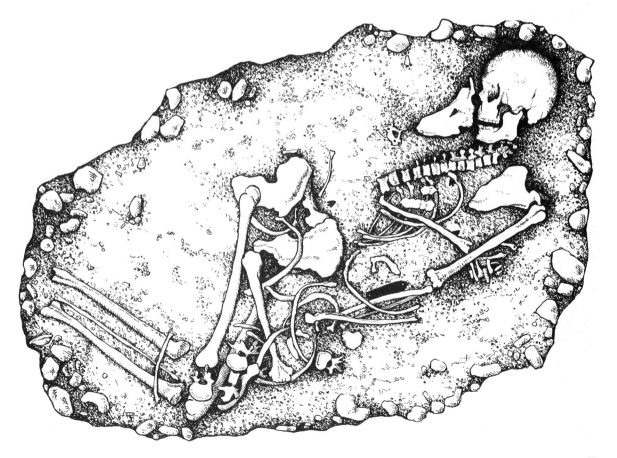

57 *Stonehenge from the south-west facing along the axis of symmetry. The low earthwork ditches and banks of the first, straight section of the Avenue can be seen running out from the Heel Stone (by the modern road) (Mick Aston).*

isolation as it now appears. In Stonehenge Bottom the Avenue seems to be aligned on a small mound, at which point it turns and runs eastwards up onto the King Barrow Ridge before sweeping south-east to the River Avon at West Amesbury.

The date of Stonehenge

Having described the elements, both visible and hidden, that make up the structure of the complete Stonehenge, the question of their date, and consequently their sequence, still remains. There are three basic ways in which either an absolute date or an idea of relative sequence, can be achieved. Firstly, radiocarbon dating will provide an absolute date of varying reliability that can be calibrated to an approx-

imation of calendar years. The radiocarbon dates available for both Stonehenge and its Avenue will be discussed below (and see **6**). Secondly, artefacts, dated elsewhere by association with radiocarbon samples, can be used to date by association. Finally, the sequence of identifiable events, if not the dates at which they occurred, can be ascertained by careful observation and recording during excavation.

A visit to the Stonehenge gallery in the Salisbury and South Wiltshire Museum will rapidly demonstrate that, for all its spectacular construction, Stonehenge was not a rich site in terms of artefacts. With the exception of the Aubrey Holes, excavated examples of which contained a range of objects dating broadly to the later part of the Neolithic period, artefacts cannot be used to provide comparative dates for any of the elements of Stonehenge described above. Dating, and consequent attempts at understanding the sequence of construction,

58 *Professor Atkinson's sequence of construction at Stonehenge.*

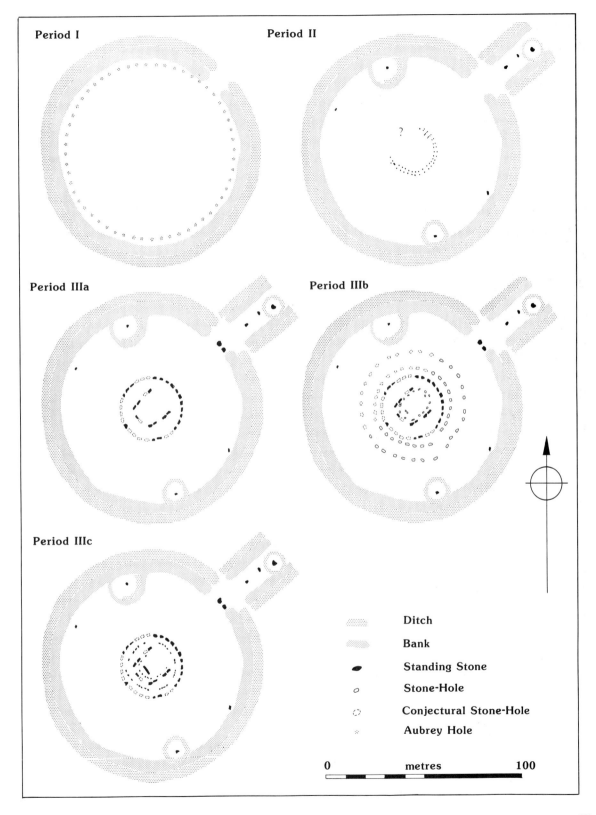

Period I

Period II

Period IIIa

Period IIIb

Period IIIc

?

Ditch

Bank

Standing Stone

Stone-Hole

Conjectural Stone-Hole

Aubrey Hole

0   metres   100

therefore rely entirely on a small number of radiocarbon dates and an even smaller number of observed relationships.

A detailed sequence of construction was originally proposed by Professor Atkinson during the course of the excavations he conducted in the 1950s. This sequence (58), originally published in *Stonehenge* in 1956, has been little modified in the intervening years, the main revision being in the dating of the enclosure ditch from more recently obtained radiocarbon samples. In the absence of a definitive excavation report presenting the evidence on which the sequence was based, it must remain the basis for our understanding of the dating of the monument. The analysis of the original findings of the excavations may help to revise or refine the sequence, the main points of which are summarized here.

The sequence of construction

One point on which all seem to agree, is that the construction of the ditch and bank marks the first phase of Stonehenge, an event which radiocarbon dates from the bottom of the ditch place around 2800 BC. Environmental evidence suggests that the enclosure was built in a cleared area, but that shortly afterwards the site itself, if not the surrounding area, was abandoned and became much overgrown. Not forgetting the 'possible timber building', this is all that can be positively identified for this first phase, although the traditional scheme also includes both the Station Stones and the Aubrey Holes.

The dating of the Aubrey Holes and their consequent inclusion at an early stage of the monument is based both on artefacts and on a single radiocarbon date. Although the much quoted date is so imprecise that it cannot be calibrated, the artefacts, particularly a number of bone pins and flint 'fabricators' do suggest a date in the later Neolithic, some time around 2200 BC. The cremations found cut into the upper levels of the Aubrey Holes also provide an indirect link with the sequence of deposits in the enclosure ditch. Here Hawley found about 30 cremations, both in the filling of the ditch and in the area of the bank. An indication that these might have been deposited over a relatively long period of time is provided by the position of those within the ditch, as they range from one example found lying on the

floor of the ditch to others in both the middle and higher levels of the silting. The Station Stones sit even more uneasily in this first phase as they are not positively dated and, where observed, their relationship with the Aubrey Holes indicated that they post-date these features. In fact, their inclusion at this early stage of the monument is largely on the basis of their apparent accurate geometrical relationship to each other, the surveying of which would have been more difficult (but not impossible) with the central stones in place. The Station Stones must consequently be regarded as so far undated on the evidence currently available.

The first Stonehenge thus appears to be a later Neolithic enclosed cemetery, constructed around 2800-2700 BC and used, possibly even in a state of semi-dereliction, for several hundred years. None of the layers and features from this early phase appear to contain chips of either sarsen or bluestone, suggesting that these stones either were not present at Stonehenge at this stage, or, if present, were not being shaped.

From this point onwards the sequence of construction becomes far more difficult to unravel and the dating evidence far more imprecise. The few available radiocarbon dates (see 6) suggest a phase of construction between 2000 and 1500 BC, but do not allow any more precise definition. This broad phase is almost totally devoid of artefacts that could be used for comparative dating and the sequence of events hinges on a very small number of observed relationships, such as where stone-holes can be shown to be cut by later stone-holes. Such relationships cannot indicate the time gap between these events however, and certainly cannot help to divide up the complex series of events which now appear to take place.

One event which can be firmly dated however, is the realignment of the entrance to the earthwork enclosure, and the associated construction of the first straight section of the Avenue. On the basis of radiocarbon dates from the ditch of the Avenue close to Stonehenge, this took place in around 2000 BC. The modification and enhancement of the enclosure entrance firmly establishes the 'axis of symmetry' on which the stone settings are aligned and which provides the potential for the observation and marking of the midsummer sunrise/midwinter sunset. The 'paired' Heel Stones are also suggested as belonging to this phase.

In the interior of the enclosure the picture is not quite so clear, though the realignment of the enclosure entrance is suggested as belonging to the same phase as the construction of the later dismantled double bluestone circle. This is dated by radiocarbon to a broadly similar date, although some doubt must be thrown upon this date as it is provided by material from a stone-hole which may not be a part of the wider arrangement. Whatever the form and date of the arrangement of bluestone 'dumb-bells', the component stones were removed and subsequently re-utilized in the bluestone circle and horseshoe.

The construction of the sarsen circle and horseshoe is suggested by Professor Atkinson as forming a separate, but chronologically indistinguishable, phase, the dating for which is provided by a single radiocarbon date of around 1900 BC. This date, however, is provided by an antler pick, the exact provenance of which does not necessarily link it with the construction of the structure that it is intended to date. A single Heel Stone, rather than the pair of the preceding phase, is suggested as standing beyond the enclosure entrance, now marked by two upright stones, one of which survives today as the recumbent Slaughter Stone.

Whatever the precise date of the sarsen structures, if they are indeed contemporaneous, they do not appear to have undergone any re-arrangement after their initial erection. This is suggested as being far from the case with the smaller, and therefore potentially more moveable bluestones. Apparently removed from site after their first arrangement in the incomplete double circle, some of them are now suggested as making a re-appearance in an oval setting within the sarsen horseshoe. The exact plan of this setting is acknowledged as being uncertain, as few of its component stone-holes have been recorded in excavation. In whatever form it may have existed, it is suggested by Professor Atkinson as having included at least two miniature bluestone trilithons, as well as a 'composite stone' made up of two individual bluestones linked together by a vertical tongue-and-groove joint (55). The evidence for the trilithons has already been described (see p.61), but whether or not they stood in this

phase, or indeed at this site, is still a matter for conjecture. The bluestones in the oval setting are also suggested as having been moved before their final arrangement in the settings that can be seen today. At this time, somewhere around 1500 BC, the 'Y' and 'Z' holes are suggested as having been dug to hold the bluestones, reverting to the original idea of a double circle. Whether or not this was ever the intention is uncertain, but the holes appear never to have held any uprights of either stone or timber.

This effectively marks the end of the arrangement and re-arrangement which took place in the centre of the enclosure in the centuries between 2000 and 1500 BC. The sequence appears to start with the realignment of the enclosure, the construction of the first stage of the Avenue, and possibly the simultaneous erection of the sarsen circle and horseshoe. The date of the first appearance of the bluestones is still far from certain, as is the nature of their arrangements prior to that which survives today. It does appear though, that the shuffling of a large number of 4 tonne stones was a simple task to those who had conceived and constructed the massive sarsen trilithons.

Although the henge itself appears to have been completed by around 1500 BC, its continuing use is suggested by the extension of the Avenue at a much later date. From the end of the first straight section in Stonehenge Bottom it takes a turn to the east, crosses over the King Barrow Ridge and finally heads off in a south-easterly direction to join the River Avon at West Amesbury. Where cut by the construction of the A303, excavations by Faith Vatcher provided a radiocarbon date of around 1200-1000 BC, on the basis of which the later extension of the Avenue was suggested. This date should be regarded with some suspicion, however, as it was obtained from samples of bone derived from *both* Avenue ditches.

Whatever the exact sequence of construction at the henge and whatever the dating of the final stages of its Avenue, Stonehenge exhibits a longevity which necessitates its consideration as an integral part of the prehistoric landscape over one-and-a-half millennia. The following chapters will chart the development of this prehistoric landscape.

5

Before Stonehenge: the earlier Neolithic

The development of the Stonehenge landscape

The prehistoric landscape surrounding Stonehenge, fragments of which we can occasionally see today among the roads, fences, woods and buildings of the modern landscape, is one of great complexity. Its development, over several thousand years, can only be understood by weaving together threads of information from a wide variety of sources. The individual threads can range from the observations of eighteenth century antiquaries, through the chance finds of ploughmen and shepherds, to the data generated by recent systematic fieldwork and excavation. Some may say that the available threads are too few and too varied in their apparent relevance to the overall picture to enable any understanding to be gained of the distant past. This is a pessimistic view, as careful weaving can create a valid, lifelike and understandable impression of the prehistoric inhabitants of Salisbury Plain and of the remarkable landscape they created and used.

Archaeology is the starting point as much today as in the times of Stukeley and Colt Hoare. Much of our basic understanding is derived from careful study of the material remains of the societies which created and used Stonehenge in its wider landscape. What is presented here, though, goes beyond the accumulated bare facts and must be regarded as a personal interpretation of the prehistoric past around Stonehenge. Opinion is not presented as fact, speculation as reality, although care has been taken to provide the most factually accurate basis for the interpretation which is offered.

The stages of landscape development are based on the chronological divisions outlined

in chapter 3. The Neolithic period is here divided into 'earlier' and 'later' Neolithic, broad time divisions which are appropriate for the study of widespread landscape change. The terms Early and Late Neolithic are reserved for more specifically dated events or forms of artefact. A similar approach is adopted for the Bronze Age, where the divisions of what is basically the majority of the second millennium BC generally rely heavily on changes in form and decoration of pottery and of metalwork. Again, such detailed chronological schemes are inappropriate for this landscape study, and broader divisions of time are employed.

Our ability to reconstruct the prehistoric landscape and to understand some of the activities of the people who populated it depends to a large extent on a combination of circumstances that occurred at the beginning of the Neolithic period, in around 4000 BC. At this time, initially on a small scale, the concept of agriculture was introduced into the British Isles. Soon monuments requiring communal effort were constructed and, with these in place, a truly settled pattern of land use started to emerge, the imprint of which can be recognized over much of the chalklands of southern England.

Prior to these innovations, during the preceding Mesolithic (Middle Stone Age) period, the inhabitants of Salisbury Plain led a mobile existence as hunters and gatherers. Despite abundant food resources, and the availability of necessities such as water and flint for tools and weapons, settlements were unlikely to have been permanent and may have moved on a seasonal basis. Shifting patterns of settlement, particularly of groups using a limited range of portable flint tools, are difficult to recognize in the archaeological record, and there are few

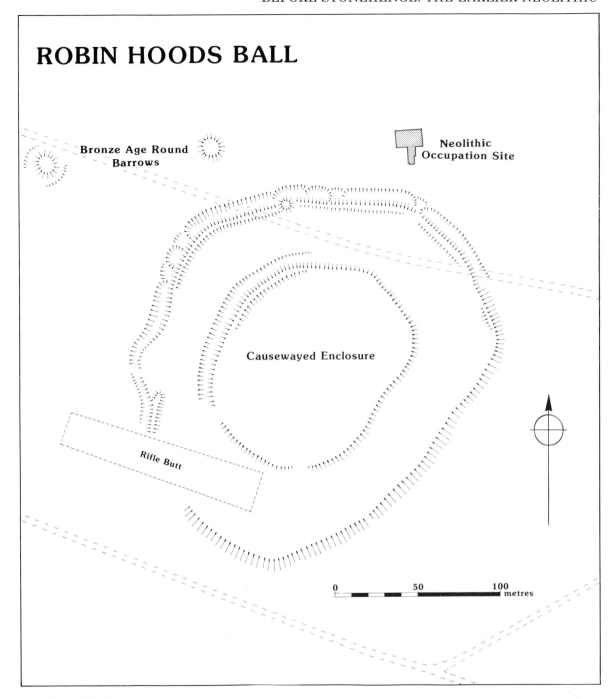

59 *Plan of Robin Hood's Ball causewayed
enclosure.*

indications that the Stonehenge area was much exploited during this period. The only positive evidence comes from three rather enigmatic pits or large post-holes which were discovered in the area of the present Stonehenge car-park during construction work in 1966. These pits, the position of which is now marked on the tarmac by concrete circles, were dated by radiocarbon as being earlier than the eighth millennium BC, and therefore pre-date even the earliest construction at Stonehenge by several thousand years.

The isolation of these pits is emphasized by the results of fieldwalking in the area, which has provided virtually no evidence of contemporary settlement. It is possible that settlement, if it did exist within this area, may have been concentrated within the nearby valleys of the Rivers Till and Avon, areas which would have offered the widest variety of natural food resources. About 24 km (15 miles) to the north, the valley of the River Kennet, which runs east from Avebury into Berkshire provides evidence of a long and rich phase of Mesolithic activity, based on plentiful supplies of fish, wild fowl and game. Here the evidence appears to show a degree of reluctance to abandon the hunter-gatherer existence, entirely understandable in an area of such natural abundance.

A further contrast with the Stonehenge area is provided by the Avebury region where small-scale clearance of woodland can be suggested as taking place in the pre-Neolithic landscape. This piecemeal clearance eventually results in the development of a mosaic of clearings, a pattern significant in the gradual opening of the landscape. This appears to be far from the case in the Stonehenge area, where the changes which characterize the beginnings of the Neolithic period probably took place in a landscape little modified by the activities of hunters and gatherers.

The monuments of the earlier Neolithic period, constructed by communal effort, provide the most obvious evidence for changes in economy, and consequently in social organization. Within the Stonehenge area the monumental framework for this period is provided by the causewayed enclosure of Robin Hood's Ball, by

60 *Pottery, animal bones and flint tools, the remains of an Early Neolithic feast in the Coneybury 'Anomaly'.*

ten long barrows of varying size and form, and by one long mortuary enclosure. There are few available radiocarbon dates for these monuments, but it is unlikely that many of them date from very much earlier than around 3500 BC.

Robin Hood's Ball

The causewayed enclosure of Robin Hood's Ball lies on the crest of a low chalk ridge about 5km (3 miles) to the north-west of Stonehenge and just within the boundaries of the Salisbury Plain Training Area (SPTA). On this part of the Plain, areas of rough grassland are primarily used for artillery practice and for the movement of heavy vehicles. This land-use has provided the enclosure, consisting of two irregularly-shaped circuits of ditches and banks (**59**), protection from the pressures of modern cultivation, and the earthworks are largely well preserved. Despite this the interior of the enclosure has until very recently been bisected by a much-used tank track and the low banks show much evidence of both past and recent trench digging by soldiers on exercise. Less recent military activity is represented by the remains of an earthen rifle butt which partly overlies the enclosure in the south. This is extremely confusing to the inexperienced prehistorian as it strongly resembles a very regular long barrow.

In the early 1960s small-scale excavations carried out by Nicholas Thomas provided evidence that the enclosure had been constructed in an area not long cleared of its woodland cover. Examination of the soil buried by the bank suggested that insufficient time had elapsed to allow a true grassland to develop. However, within this new clearing there was clear evidence for the establishment of a settlement prior to the construction of the enclosure. Sherds of pottery, scatters of charcoal and post-holes were recorded from beneath the outer enclosure bank suggesting a focus of settlement, the true extent of which was only demonstrated by more recent fieldwork. In 1984 an area of previously undisturbed grassland to the east of the causewayed enclosure was ploughed, possibly for the first time since the Roman period, revealing scatters of flint tools and, more surprisingly, considerable quantities of prehistoric pottery dating from the Early Neolithic to the Late Bronze Age. One very well-defined scatter of flint tools, including many

61 *Pottery and evidence for cereal processing from the Coneybury 'Anomaly' (Jane Brayne).*

scrapers, together with Early Neolithic pottery, lay very close to the causewayed enclosure and, on excavation, was found to overlie a group of pits dug into the underlying chalk. These contained animal bone, pottery, flint tools and other domestic debris, radiocarbon dated to around 3200-3000 BC. The pottery includes both locally produced wares and, significantly, sherds of the gabbroic wares from the Lizard area of Cornwall. Such 'exotic' pottery suggests that those who first cleared the area, and who subsequently constructed the causewayed enclosure, were part of wide networks of trade and exchange within which such enclosures may have played an important part.

All the evidence from around Robin Hood's Ball suggests a community that had embraced a relatively settled way of life. The animal bones include a large proportion of those from domesticated stock, mainly cattle, pig and the occasional sheep, and there is clearly sufficient social organization for the considerable task of constructing the enclosure to be planned and executed.

The Coneybury 'Anomaly'

A contrast to this apparently settled existence can be seen in the contents of a remarkable pit discovered and excavated in 1980 as part of the Stonehenge Environs Project. The pit would not have been discovered had it not lain close to the henge monument on Coneybury Hill, where it was noted as a large and discrete magnetic anomaly on the geophysical survey carried out prior to the excavation of the henge (see **37**). In recognition of the way in which it first came to be noticed the pit became known as the Coneybury 'Anomaly', a name which has persisted. On excavation it was found to date to the Early Neolithic period, a single radiocarbon sample suggesting that the pit was filled in around 3850 BC, and to contain a primary deposit of almost solid pottery, animal bones and flint (**60**). The 1375 sherds of pottery represent at least 41 vessels, ranging from small cups to large cooking or serving pots (**61**). Some of the larger vessels, with lugs and rolled-over rims, both of which would enable hide covers to be attatched, could also have been used for storage purposes. The closest modern analogy for this exciting collection of pottery is with a punch set, for mixing and serving drinks. There certainly is evidence for social eating, if not for drinking, in the large quantities of animal bones recovered with the pottery. Over 2000 fragments were excavated, mainly of cattle and roe deer, with smaller numbers of pig, red deer, beaver and fish. Together these bones represent a major episode of butchery in which at least ten cattle, several roe deer, one pig and two red deer were processed. Of this huge quantity of meat, only that from the roe deer was apparently eaten at this time, however, the rest probably being taken away for later consumption.

All the evidence points to the contents of this pit representing the accumulated debris from either a single major feast, or from a series of feasts. On the basis of the evidence of immature animals, the feasting appears to have taken place during the summer months, but for what purpose is less certain. The type of pottery contained within the pit, while remarkable in quantity, lacks any of the more 'exotic' types, such as the gabbroic pottery from Cornwall. This is commonly found in the causewayed enclosures of similar date and the link between a more sedentary, and at least partly agriculturally-based lifestyle, involvement in the developing trade networks along which certain types

of pottery and other goods moved, and the construction of monuments, has been noted above (see p. 23). In contrast, the evidence from the 'Anomaly' points to a more mobile economy, still Mesolithic in many ways. The worked flints from this pit include a greater proportion of blades, themselves indicative of a mobile lifestyle, and the animal bones are evidence of a still considerable exploitation of wild animals, with some lingering emphasis on the nearby river valleys shown by the bones of beaver and of fish. It is possible that those who dug the pit were excluded from the formalities of the causewayed enclosure nearby, the rituals of its

62 *Plan of the Normanton Down long mortuary enclosure (after Vatcher 1961).*

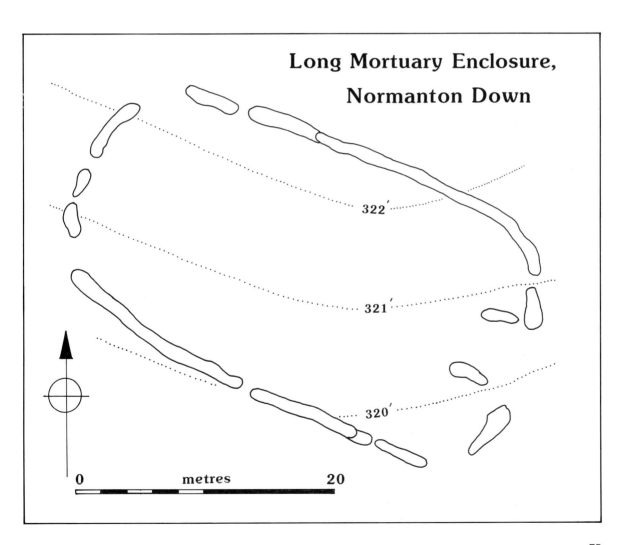

construction and use and the trading privileges that acccompanied it. Perhaps the digging of a large pit as a receptacle for their feasting debris represents the only permanent record of the presence of these more mobile exploiters of the Stonehenge landscape in the Early Neolithic.

Long barrows
The desire to settle and to establish territory was, however, obviously present in this period. As already suggested, long barrows are often considered to be as much territorial statements as receptacles for the dead. If this suggestion is accepted, then the area of Salisbury Plain on which Stonehenge was later to be built may have been the subject of territorial disputes. At least ten long barrows were built, of widely varying size. The largest, at over 80 m (264 ft) is the one which formed the focus for the Winterbourne Stoke 'crossroads' round barrow group, (see **18**) while at the other end of the scale, Wilsford 13, within the Normanton Down barrow group, is barely 20 m (66 ft) long. This range of size corresponds at least partly with a variety of forms. The more massive examples, suggested as earlier in date, consist of a mound flanked by quarry ditches (see **8**), while the shorter examples often show signs of ditches which continue in a 'U' shape around the shallower and narrower end of the long mound. Often grouped together under the confusing name of 'short' long barrows, a distinct cluster can be seen to the south-west of Stonehenge on the Stonehenge, Normanton and Wilsford Downs. Although no evidence of date is available for any of the examples within this group, they may be later in date than the more traditional long barrows and may consequently be more firmly associated with the following phase of Neolithic monument construction, within which the cursus monuments were constructed.

Unlike the long barrows of, for example, the Avebury area, those within the Stonehenge Environs have received little attention from excavators, both antiquarian and recent. Early excavators such as Colt Hoare realized that long barrows provided little in the way of material grave goods, and that their excavation required considerable effort. Later in the nineteenth century Thurnham, an archaeologist with a greater interest in bones than in grave goods, excavated several examples, including Amesbury 42, the barrow at the eastern end

of the Stonehenge Cursus. Within Wiltshire however, his preference, hardly surprisingly was for those areas where the mounds of the long barrows covered stone burial chambers. This made his work considerably easier.

In recent years only one long barrow has been investigated, a newly discovered example at Netheravon Bake, just to the north-east of Robin Hood's Ball. Once again, ploughing of a long-standing area of grassland revealed the site, this time as a soil mark, the ditches showing dark in contrast to the white chalk. In plan Netheravon Bake resembles a 'short' long barrow, and could therefore be expected to be relatively late in the overall dating sequence of long barrows. It is surprising then, that excavations carried out as part of the Stonehenge Environs Project showed that there were at least two Neolithic phases, the earliest of which dates to around 3500 BC, after which the remains of the earlier monument were remodelled as a round barrow in the earlier Bronze Age.

In 1959 an unusual type of site, but one which needs to be considered alongside long barrows, was excavated on Normanton Down. This was a 'long mortuary enclosure', first recorded on an aerial photograph. The ground plan recovered by excavation (**62**) showed an elongated enclosure defined by discontinuous ditches which originally had an external bank. At the eastern end, by an apparent entrance, were a pair of short, parallel bedding trenches, each of which had originally contained three upright posts supported by horizontal timbers. Although the appearance of the overall site cannot even be guessed at, this entrance structure may best be interpreted as a possible portal. A radiocarbon date in the late fourth millennium BC places the enclosure in the centre of the date range for conventional long barrows.

Earlier Neolithic settlement
The monuments described above provide clear evidence of the investment of considerable amounts of labour in the Stonehenge area in the earlier Neolithic. Areas of woodland must have been cleared, if only to provide open spaces within which the construction of enclosures and long barrows was to take place (**colour plate 3**). These are unlikely to be the only cleared areas though, and the evidence available suggests that additional clearance for

cultivation was also taking place. If long barrows are accepted as indicative of the need for territorial demarcation, then pressure on land would seem to be indicated at a very early stage of settlement, settlement for which until recently there was very little direct evidence.

Prior to recent survey work, only limited evidence for earlier Neolithic activity beyond the confines of the monuments described above had been recorded in the form of isolated artefacts and archaeological deposits. The former tend to be casual finds of more easily recognizable tools, the occurrence of which tends to correspond with areas of intensive recent cultivation. The distribution of these finds also demonstrates the results of concentrated fieldwork on one specific area, in this case the King Barrow Ridge. Here, during the 1930s, the pioneering fieldwork carried out by Laidler and Young produced huge quantities of flint tools, indicating an extensive area of both earlier and later Neolithic activity.

The importance of this area can also be demonstrated by the consistent occurrence of pits and spreads of occupation material of earlier Neolithic date. These have been recovered both in excavations from beneath round barrows of much later date and in observations during improvements to the A303 road. The pattern of continuity apparent on the King Barrow Ridge can be seen to occur also at Durrington Walls, where inextensive excavations in 1966 and 1967 showed that the Late Neolithic enclosure had been built in an area already much used. Plain earlier Neolithic pottery, a ground flint axe and leaf-shaped arrowheads, were recovered from under the bank in both areas examined, but primarily in the northern cutting. Radiocarbon dates from both bank cuttings suggest an area of extensive and potentially mobile settlement, spanning a period in the second half of the fourth millennium BC, and apparently focused on the valley of the River Avon.

The scattered earlier Neolithic pits on which much of our understanding of this phase of settlement has to be based, contain artefacts which appear to be of a purely domestic nature. The animal bones are primarily of domestic stock, although there is still evidence that wild animals were hunted, and the small quantities of pottery can all be identified as local products. Viewed in isolation, it is difficult to suggest the initial function of these pits, and only in rare cases do scatters of surface artefacts provide any sort of a context, indicating the extent of the settlement activity of which the pits are only a part. Within the Stonehenge area, as is the case in any other area with a similar agricultural history, the identification of areas of earlier Neolithic activity cannot depend entirely on the recovery of pottery from the surface of ploughed fields. Although easily identifiable, pottery of this period is also extremely fragile and will not survive the effects of repeated ploughing or exposure to frost. Identification must therefore also depend on the recognition and collection of a range of flint tools, more robust but in many cases less precisely datable. Leaf-shaped arrowheads and ground flint axes are the most positive and unambiguous tool types, but certain forms of the more common flint scrapers can also be suggested as dating to this period.

Despite the problems of interpreting the results from surface collection, with fields possibly containing scatters of artefacts representing a range of activities spread over two or more millennia, it is possible to suggest a number of areas within the Stonehenge landscape which offer positive evidence for different types of human activity and land use.

The results of recent surface collection on the King Barrow Ridge have provided confirmation of the significance of the previous discoveries mentioned above. Evidence for extensive earlier Neolithic activity occurs in the form of many ground flint axes, both whole and fragmentary, the broken examples possibly damaged in use. This concentration of axes appears to be relatively restricted and occurs mainly in the area later crossed by the Stonehenge Avenue. The emphasis on the ridge is continued south onto Coneybury Hill, where dense scatters of flint scrapers of an earlier Neolithic type have been recovered. To the east, close to the River Avon, the evidence from surface collection suggests that occupation recorded at Durrington Walls may not be extensive, and in fact may be restricted to the edge of the river valley, a pattern repeated close to the River Avon near West Amesbury.

Within the area defined by the valley of the River Avon and Stonehenge Bottom, the combined evidence from excavation, fieldwalking and chance finds suggests a range of activities designed to exploit the resources offered by a variety of zones. The river valley was a rich resource area and could perhaps offer sufficient potential for the development of more stable areas of settled activity on its margins. This is possibly how we should view the pre-enclosure settlement at Durrington Walls, where environmental evidence suggests that a phase of woodland clearance may also be associated with cultivation during the earlier Neolithic period. Whether or not cultivation took place, it is clear that considerable investment was made in extensive clearance, perhaps representing the creation and maintenance of a base area from which more mobile and sporadic exploitation of the chalk to the east was carried out. Such exploitation could involve the creation and maintenance of areas of grassland, the King Barrow Ridge perhaps forming the boundary between two ecological zones, one relatively open, the other, to the west of the

ridge, still largely wooded.

To the west, beyond the area of the King Barrow Ridge, there is evidence for earlier Neolithic activity, possibly settlement of a rather more sporadic type, concentrated in three specific areas. The most defined of these lies between Winterbourne Stoke Crossroads and Wilsford Down, an area containing the most coherent cluster of long barrows within the Stonehenge area, six examples within an area of less than 200 ha (480 acres). Within this area, in contrast to the evidence from the surface of the King Barrow Ridge, finds of earlier Neolithic flint tools consist primarily of scrapers, perhaps indicative of differing types of activity. This pattern is repeated on Stonehenge Down and again, this time over a wider area, in fields located to the north of the Cursus.

6

The developing Neolithic

The monuments discussed so far, and the slender evidence for contemporary settlement activity, belong primarily within the first half of the fourth millennium BC. All are associated with plain, round-bottomed pottery and a range of flint tools including ground axes and leaf-shaped arrowheads, forms which may continue in use well into the third millennium BC. At this time, however, they overlap with new and distinctive styles of pottery, initially highly-decorated Peterborough wares, followed shortly by the often equally exuberant Grooved Ware (see **14**). These innovations in pottery styles, together with changes in the range of flint tools now found, can be broadly associated with the appearance of novel types of monument. The new monuments and the new artefacts, infrequently found in association, characterize a rather nebulous period, the 'Middle Neolithic', formerly seen as a time of hiatus, but now, in the light of more recent archaeological research, seen as a period when profound and far-reaching social changes may be taking place. It is possible that the effects

of stresses which caused conflict in the earlier Neolithic, competition for both land and resources and even as a result of over-population, may continue to be strongly felt in the developing Neolithic society.

It is during this period that the final flourish of the concept of linear monuments can be seen. Previously epitomized by long barrows, two extremes now develop: 'short' long barrows, already mentioned (p. 76) where long monuments now appear in a contracted form, and cursus monuments, the opposite extreme.

There are, within the Stonehenge Environs, two examples of this new and strange variation.

The Stonehenge Cursus
The best-known, larger and nowadays more accessible example is the Stonehenge Cursus, an enormously elongated ditched enclosure, an average of over 100m (330 ft) wide and 2.8km (over 2 miles) long (**63**). Aligned in an east-

63 *Plan of the Stonehenge Cursus.*

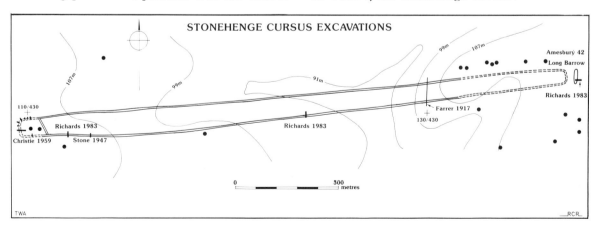

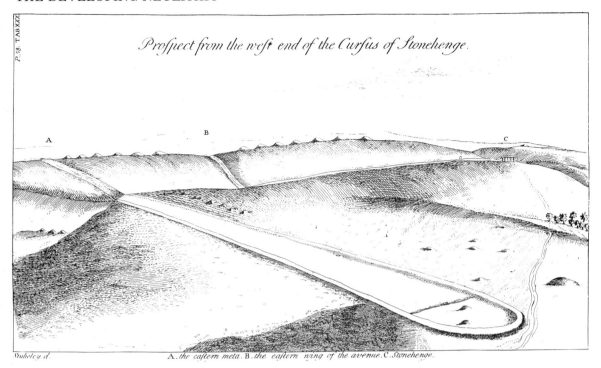

Profpect from the weft end of the Curfus of Stonehenge.

Stukeley d.   *A. the eaftern meta. B. the eaftern wing of the avenue. C. Stonehenge.*

64 *The Stonehenge Cursus engraved by William Stukeley in 1723. This 'prospect' shows the Cursus with a rounded western terminal, contradicting the evidence both on the ground and in his own preliminary sketches.*

west direction just to the north of Stonehenge over the crest of a Down, the monument was originally discovered by William Stukeley in 1723. Set in a landscape at that time untouched by cultivation, sufficient survived of the enclosure for Stukeley to be able to record its full extent in several drawn prospects (**64**). He was also able to note that the banks at either end were considerably larger than those which defined its sides, a configuration which helped Stukeley towards his interpretation of this strange new monument. It was obvious that he had discovered a racecourse, a 'Cursus', or 'hippodrome', of Roman date and built for the purpose of chariot racing. The end banks were clearly provided for the benefit of the spectators, and it is tempting to speculate that the reasons for changes in the appearance of the monument between Stukeley's field drawings and those which were finally published, were to accommodate this theory. After all it would

be easier for the chariots to make a high-speed turn at the western end if that end were gently rounded, instead of squared off as it is in reality, and as Stukeley originally drew it.

Until relatively recently, it was difficult to appreciate the scale and layout of the Stonehenge Cursus, landscape changes in the centuries since Stukeley's original observations having either levelled or obscured much of the monument. The low side banks for almost the entire eastern half had been levelled by cultivation, and the outfall from a sewage works cuts across the monument in the shallow dry valley which marks the lowest point between the gentle ridges on which both terminals lie. At the eastern terminal, in the position shown by Stukeley, lies Amesbury long barrow 42, now barely recognizable with a bridle road along the mound, one ditch in an arable field and the other in a recent plantation. Some idea of the original scale of the barrow was revealed in 1983 when a single trench was excavated across the line of the ditch which lies within the arable field. Not only was the main quarry ditch of substantial proportions, nearly 3m (10 ft) deep and over 5m (16½ ft) wide at the surface (**65**), but an earlier ditch was also located. This was much smaller and, within the confines of the excavation trench, showed

(top right)

3 The earlier Neolithic landscape around Stonehenge. Viewed from the King Barrow Ridge, the landscape shortly after 3000 BC would have revealed the first phase of Stonehenge, together with scattered long barrows and cursus monuments lying within small, but rapidly expanding, woodland clearings (Jane Brayne).

(above)

4 In the later Neolithic period the woodland resources of the Stonehenge landscape were dwindling, necessitating careful management. Coppicing provided a renewable source of sturdy wooden stakes for fuel and building, while woodland pasture may have supported herds of grazing pigs (Jane Brayne).

(bottom right)

5 The Early Bronze Age landscape around Stonehenge. In about 2000 BC sheep grazed extensive areas of established pasture, at the centre of which Stonehenge was rebuilt and the first stage of the Avenue constructed. At the same time great cemeteries of round barrows appeared on many of the low surrounding hill tops (Jane Brayne).

(top left)

6 The barrow cemetery at Winterbourne Stoke Crossroads is the most remarkable within the Stonehenge Environs, not only for its state of preservation, but also for its diversity of barrow types. A large Neolithic long barrow forms the focus for the Bronze Age cemetery, which includes bowl, bell, saucer, disc and pond barrows (Mick Aston).

(bottom left)

7 The best surviving section of the sarsen circle viewed from the north-east. On gently tapering uprights lie curved lintels, jointed end-to-end and providing some indication of the appearance of the continuous ring of stone that they originally formed (English Heritage).

(above)

8 The bluestone circle. Lying concentric to the sarsen circle (the interior view of the section seen in colour plate 7) the bluestones show a marked contrast with the sarsens both in overall size and in irregularity of shape (English Heritage).

(left)
9 The ruins of the Great Trilithon. The tallest sarsen, on which the projecting tenon can clearly be seen, is nearly 7m (22ft) high. In front of it, with its corresponding mortice holes, lies the lintel which fell in 1797 (English Heritage).

(above)
10 The last part of the journey from Wales: the bluestones rafted up the River Avon (Jane Brayne).

(right)
11 At the end of the Bronze Age the then ancient Stonehenge lay within an increasingly agricultural landscape. The henge itself was surrounded by grassland, beyond which lay fields and farms, barrows and boundaries, together representing the last prehistoric landscape of the area which we can reconstruct with any certainty (Jane Brayne).

12 The spectacular gold finds excavated by Cunnington from the Bush Barrow. The decorated sheet gold lozenges and belt hook would have been powerful symbols of wealth to their wearer (see colour plate 13).

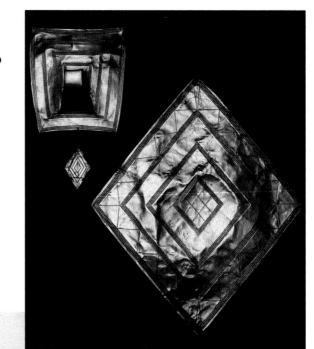

13 The Bush Barrow 'warrior' at Stonehenge. Clearly a person of great power, outwardly symbolized by gold ornaments, gold-handled daggers, a 'sceptre' and possibly a shield and spear (Jane Brayne).

evidence of a causeway. Was this the original end of the Cursus, which now appears to stop short of the long barrow mound? Only further investigation will tell.

The excavation of the earlier ditch provided a rare insight into the methods of working of an individual Neolithic flint-knapper. A tightly-defined cluster of flint flakes and cores was found lying on the base of the ditch, the result of perhaps only a few minutes of knapping, but undisturbed for nearly 5000 years.

Unfortunately the western terminal of the Cursus has also had a varied and disturbed history. Lying beyond the protection offered by the planting of Fargo Wood in the 1840s, the earthworks were encroached upon by buildings before finally being levelled for cultivation in

65 *The eastern flanking ditch of Amesbury 42 long barrow revealed by excavation in 1983. The small hollow on the left is the earlier causewayed ditch. The larger ditch on the right is the second phase ditch which must have provided chalk for a substantial mound.*

the 1940s, with Stukeley's 'grandstand' banks pushed down into the silted ditch.

Over the last decade subtle changes have taken place in the management of the land on which the Stonehenge Cursus lies, changes designed to enhance the understanding of the monument and its position within the overall prehistoric landscape. Fences have in some cases been removed, in others simply moved to mark the position of a levelled section of the ditch and bank. An area of Fargo Wood has been felled to define clearly the width of the Cursus, particularly striking when viewed from the eastern end. Within this cleared area a small excavation in 1983 not only demonstrated the small size of the side ditch, but also showed that here the apparent low bank was merely a 'ghost', a rise in the surface of the natural chalk marking the bank's former position (**66**). More recently the remains of the western terminal have been reconstructed to the state that they were in prior to the recent but drastic episode of levelling (**67**).

These attempts to reconstruct some of the visual impact that a monument of this size

66 Excavation of the southern side ditch of the Stonehenge Cursus in 1983, carried out within an area only recently cleared of trees. The 'ghost' bank can be seen in the slight rise in the level of the chalk beyond the ditch.

must originally have possessed could be greatly assisted by a firm knowledge of its function and purpose. The limited investigations that have been carried out so far have failed to provide the required answers to such fundamental questions. Since the first archaeological observation, by Percy Farrer who observed the cutting of a military pipe trench during the First World War, the Cursus has been the subject of limited excavation on a number of occasions (see **63**). The majority of the excavations have examined the southern flanking ditch and bank, the only exception being those carried out by Patricia Christie on the western terminal in 1959. These excavations have emphasized the difference in profile between the side and terminal ditches, and more recently, have provided both data for environmental analysis and samples for radiocarbon dating. We can now be certain that the monument is not Roman but Neolithic in date, but beyond this Stukeley could be

at least partly correct in his interpretation. Remove the idea of the chariots and the Cursus would have formed an ideal setting for processions, games, races, a wide range of potential activities, all virtually irrecoverable from the archaeological record.

The Lesser Cursus

The Lesser Cursus, a smaller example of this type of monument, lies on the crest of a low ridge to the north-west of Stonehenge. No longer visible at ground level, its true form can only be discerned from soil or crop marks visible on aerial photographs (**68**). These show a ditched enclosure approximately 400m (1320 ft) in length, the western end formed as a regular terminal, but with the ditches at the opposite end apparently stopping, leaving the enclosure open-ended. The Lesser Cursus is also bisected by a central cross-ditch, leaving the sequence of construction and modification uncertain. Was it originally shorter? Has it been extended? Was it left unfinished? Some of these questions were answered by sample excavation of three areas carried out in 1983.

Excavation at the eastern end examined one of the ditches which was shown to come to an apparently deliberate end. The evidence from surface parch marks visible in the grass during a very hot summer, and confirmed by geophysical survey, suggested that a similar regularity could be expected from the other, unexamined eastern ditch terminal. In contrast, the ditch at the western 'closed' end was considerably larger, its filling showing a complicated sequence of events. These included re-cutting the ditch when it was partly silted up, after which the final episode involved the deliberate pushing in of the bank into what by that time must have been a shallow depression.

Perhaps the most informative area, however, was that excavated at the junction of the internal cross-ditch with that of the southern side of the cursus. This revealed a complex of ditches (**69**) the excavation of which showed a clear sequence of events and which provided suitable material for radiocarbon dating. The first version of the Lesser Cursus apparently ended at this point and was consequently around 200m (660 ft) in length. The enclosure was defined by a very small ditch with an internal bank, and was built around 3000 BC. Subsequently this small enclosure was both enlarged and extended: existing ditches were re-dug, leaving only small sections intact, and an extension was built in an easterly direction, effectively doubling its length. Very few artefacts were recovered from the excavation of the ditches, the chalky filling of which suggested deliberate back-filling, perhaps not long after they were originally dug. Positive evidence of the way in which the ditches were dug came from the bottom of one section of ditch where antler tools, picks (**70**) and rakes were laid out in an orderly and deliberate manner (**71**). This should not be regarded as the simple disposal of rubbish, but more as tangible evidence of the ceremony and ritual which surely went

67 *Reconstruction work at the western terminal of the Stonehenge Cursus in July 1990 with a completed section lying beyond the work in progress. Careful excavation has revealed the chalk of the former bank lying in the hollow of the ditch where it was bulldozed in the 1940s. The chalk will be used to reconstruct the bank in its former position.*

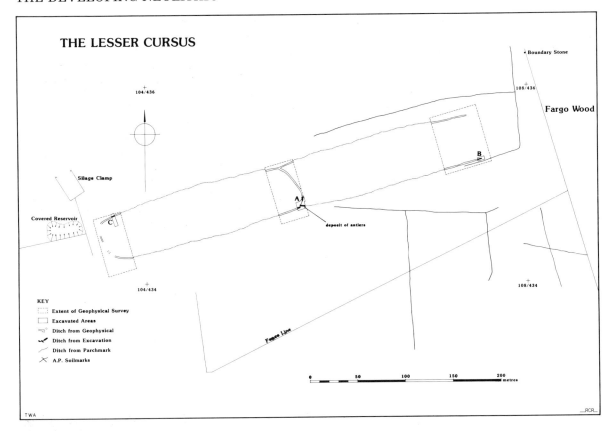

68 *Plan of the Lesser Cursus revealed by a combination of geophysical survey, parch marks in grass, and excavation.*

with the construction, as well as the use, of such an enigmatic monument.

Environmental and economic evidence

Within this 'middle' Neolithic the two cursus monuments may seem apparently isolated, their lack of association with distinctive types of pottery or flint tools making the identification of associated settlement activity a difficult process. However, recent excavations have demonstrated that such activity did occur within the Stonehenge area, and sequences of environmental evidence which span this apparently transitional period show little or no sign of a phase of abandonment and consequent dereliction. Indeed the evidence from the Stonehenge area suggests that this period is one of continuing growth which sees the development, exten-

sion and final form of a range of soon to be archaic linear monuments.

Our current understanding of the environmental background and economy of the earlier Neolithic is unfortunately based on very limited data. There is a danger that the analysis of snail assemblages from specific monuments may reflect little more than an extremely localized environmental sequence, which in many cases, hardly surprisingly, suggests that the monument was built in a cleared area. Even after the recent programme of intensive fieldwork, few deposits have been located which contain a wide range of economic data. Sufficient now exists, however, for careful analysis to provide some indication of economic and environmental trends.

Although the precise nature and extent of woodland clearance during the earlier Neolithic cannot be determined, even that which must have been necessary to allow the construction of individual monuments suggests an extensive and developing pattern of clearance (**colour plate 3**). The evidence associated with the early settlement at Durrington Walls must also be considered within this gradual opening up of the landscape, within which there is surprisingly little direct evidence for cereal cultivation. Environmental evidence from the Durrington Walls settlement hints at some cultivation and other contemporary pits recently sampled have produced small quantities of heavily-burnt cereal, the only identified type being emmer wheat. The occurrence within earlier Neolithic contexts of fragments of what appear to be querns or rubbers can also be taken as indicating cereal processing, but such stones may also have performed a similar function for wild grains or may even have been used for flint axe sharpening.

Clearly the 'Neolithic revolution' did not automatically mean an immediate shift of emphasis to a formalized cereal-based economy, a model for development that has often been suggested for this stage of prehistory. The evidence from the earlier Neolithic in the Stonehenge area suggests little progress in this direction and so, if extensive clearance is suggested, then the widespread establishment of grassland can be envisaged. The ecological requirements of both cattle and pigs are little different from those of their wild counterparts, and, within the Stonehenge area, the occurrence of both domestic cattle and to a lesser degree pig, together with wild species, suggests a continuing emphasis on the exploitation of areas of largely unmodified environment. Hazel nuts occur consistently within pits of this period, also pointing to the continuing use of scrub and woodland resources and re-emphasizing the heavy dependence of most early agricultural communities on wild food resources.

69 *A complex of ditches revealed by excavation at the Lesser Cursus in 1983. Three ditches terminate within this small area, at the mid-point of the southern side ditch (area A on **68**).*

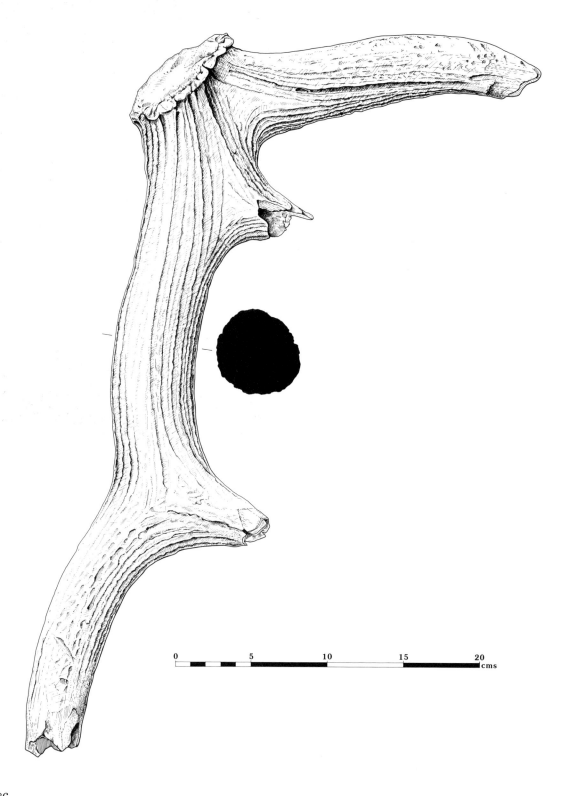

71 *Antler picks and rakes discovered on the bottom of the Lesser Cursus ditch in 1983. These tools appear to be a deliberate and carefully-placed deposit rather than merely a dump of rubbish. As such they may provide hints of the ceremonies concerned with the construction, if not the use of Cursus monuments.*

70 *An antler pick from the base of the Lesser Cursus ditch, dated by radiocarbon to around 3400 BC (Miranda Schofield).*

7

The later Neolithic

The later Neolithic period in the Stonehenge area is characterized by the appearance of a range of novel forms of earthwork enclosure, some requiring massive effort in their construction, and by the continuing development of a range of highly-decorated styles of pottery (see **25**). Despite the fact that the major monuments constructed during this period demonstrate a change in emphasis from linear forms to enclosures this should not be taken to suggest any major discontinuity with the patterns of economy and settlement developed during the earlier Neolithic. With regard to these new enclosures, an evolutionary scheme has been proposed which sees them as a direct development of the ideas embodied in the causewayed enclosures of the earlier Neolithic. This argument suggests that it is unlikely that two independent traditions would have developed, each involving the construction of substantial, but apparently non-utilitarian enclosures. Within the Stonehenge area, where the first simple enclosure phase at Stonehenge itself provides the continuity between the causewayed enclosure of Robin Hood's Ball and the later henges, this argument takes on more credibility.

Henge monuments
Within the Stonehenge Environs five enclosures of later Neolithic date can be identified. Grouped together as 'henges', they exhibit the wide range of size, shape, apparent use and date typical of this ill-matched class of monument (see p. 25). These five examples are Stonehenge (see **39**), Coneybury (see **75**), Woodhenge (see **78**) – these three regarded as 'classic henges' – the huge 'henge enclosure' of Durrington Walls (see **77**), and the tiny

'hengiform' enclosure in Fargo Plantation, now classified as a 'mini-henge' (**72**).

Of these monuments, the most anomalous, complex, and, in terms of its initial construction, the earliest, is Stonehenge. Here it has long been recognized that the circular earthwork enclosure represents the earliest definable phase of the monument, constructed in the late fourth millennium BC. This places Stonehenge I very early in the sequence of henge construction, within the same date bracket as sites at Balfarg in Fife, Llandegai in Gwynedd and Stenness in Orkney, rather than within the later Wessex Group, perhaps typified in this area by Woodhenge and Durrington Walls.

Additional elements suggested as belonging to this first phase include the excavation and rapid backfilling of the Aubrey Holes, the erection of the Heel Stone and its pair and the 'possible indeed probable' timber structure in the centre of the enclosure. Currently available information, as discussed in chapter 4, unfortunately allows only speculation about the internal structure of the enclosure, although the insertion of cremations into Aubrey Holes and into the ditch and bank suggests the possibility of an enclosed cremation cemetery. Some indication of date for this aspect of the monument is provided by the Late Neolithic objects which accompany some cremations. Of whatever form and significance, this first Stonehenge appears to have had a relatively short period of use and maintenance prior to its rapid recolonization by rank grass and scrub, firm indication of the abandonment which may have lasted for a considerable period of time.

The earliest phase of Stonehenge has little

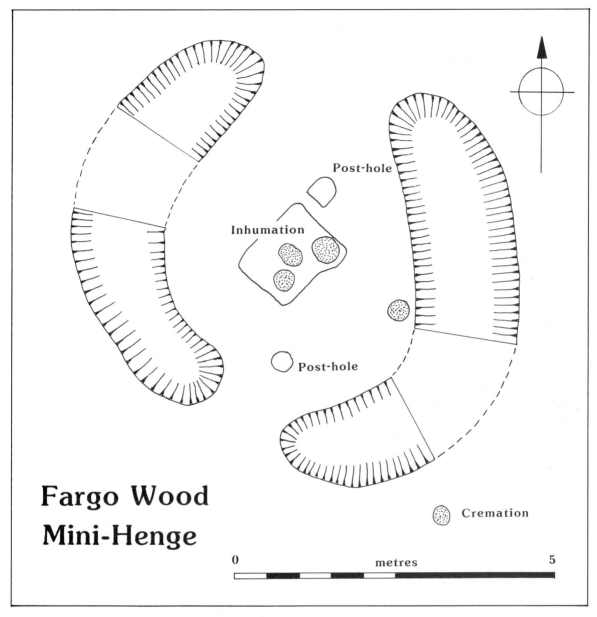

Fargo Wood Mini-Henge

Post-hole

Inhumation

Post-hole

Cremation

0   metres   5

72 *The Fargo Wood 'mini-henge' (after Stone 1938).*

in common in both form and chronology with other classic henges; although the recent excavations carried out at Coneybury have demonstrated some areas of similarity.

Coneybury Henge

Until relatively recently, the cropmark enclosure lying to the south-east of Stonehenge on Coneybury Hill was interpreted as the remains of a large, ploughed-out round barrow, although no standing earthwork barrow had been recorded here by either Stukeley or Colt Hoare. The true nature of the site was clarified by aerial photographs taken during the 1950s which showed not a circular ditch but an oval ditched enclosure with a single, north-east facing entrance. This shape, and the suggestion from the photographs of traces of an external bank, led to the reclassification of the site as a small henge monument.

73 *Environmental sampling at Coneybury Henge in 1980. Martin Bell is removing a column of soil samples from the layers filling the southern ditch. The irregular nature of the ditch bottom is plainly visible. The dark band in the ditch fill is the remains of a Bronze Age turf line and above this the white chalk layer marks the remains of the outer bank, pushed into the partly silted ditch prior to a phase of cultivation.*

After its discovery the site was given statutory protection by being scheduled as an ancient monument, but nonetheless remained under annual arable cultivation. In 1979 the Royal Commission on the Historical Monuments of England suggested the need for investigation by means of both geophysical survey and test excavation, a recommendation that was implemented in 1980. The investigation, the first stage of the Stonehenge Environs Project, was designed to provide information on the survival of the site, information vital to developing a suitable preservation policy. The excavations were also intended to be a test-bed for newly-developed techniques in survey and excavation method.

Prior to any soil disturbance, a range of geophysical surveys were carried out, producing a remarkably detailed picture of the structure of the enclosure, together with suggestions of varying activities within its interior. Magnetometer survey, in which the ditch showed up as an exceptionally strong magnetic signal (see **37**), provided an accurate plan of the major elements of the site, showing clearly such details as the single north-east facing entrance. An even stronger signal was produced by the large pit, the Coneybury 'Anomaly', lying close by to the north (see p. 74).

Within the interior of the enclosure measurements were taken of the magnetic susceptibility of the plough-soil, with higher levels perhaps indicating areas where fires had burnt in the past. Some confirmation of the effectiveness of this technique was demonstrated during the subsequent excavation of the plough-soil, where clusters of fire-cracked flints provided more tangible evidence of these areas of possible burning.

The enclosure ditch was examined in two places and, while exhibiting some broad similarity in the sequence of filling, the excavated ditch sections were very different in both plan and profile. The ditch at the southern section, about 2.5m (8 ft) deep and 5m (16½ ft) wide at ground level, had an irregular 'gang dug' appearance, and the profile at the base was narrow and 'V' shaped (**73**). The lower edges of the ditch were very fresh looking and within the chalk rubble that accumulates rapidly as the result of frost and rain shattering exposed chalk edges, lay the incomplete skeletons of a dog and of a white-tailed sea eagle, a rare bird for the Wiltshire chalk. A radiocarbon date from the base of the ditch here suggests that it was dug in around 2750 BC.

The northern section exposed a 5m (16½ ft) length of the western ditch terminal which, although of a broadly similar size to that recorded in the southern cutting, had a markedly different profile and appearance. Here the ditch was U-shaped and flat-bottomed, its sides smoothed in contrast to the jagged sides of the southern cutting (**74**). A step cut into the interior side of the ditch was perhaps to assist the original ditch diggers to get out of such a deep cutting. The appearance of the terminal ditch, together with the nature of its lower fills suggest that it may have been cleared of accumulated chalk rubble at least once before being allowed to silt up naturally.

Within the interior the excavation revealed a number of different types of features (**75**): pits, post-holes and large numbers of small and enigmatic stake-holes. In the centre of the enclosure lay a possible circle of pits or post-holes, some of which may have held upright stones or timbers, and many of which contained small quantities of Grooved Ware pottery. Beyond the pits, running concentric to the inner edge of the ditch were the remains of a circle of small posts, a circle which also incorporated two pits apparently flanking the 'axis of symmetry' of the enclosure. In the southern excavated segment at least, the post-holes exhibited a regular spacing and great similarity in dimensions and profile. The survival of such shallow features within this part of the enclosure is due largely to the buffering effect of the deeper soils which formed over the scarped interior. Presumably as part of the earthmoving associated with the major construction of the ditch and bank, the interior of the enclosure appears to have been terraced into the slight slope to form an effectively horizontal platform (**76**).

91

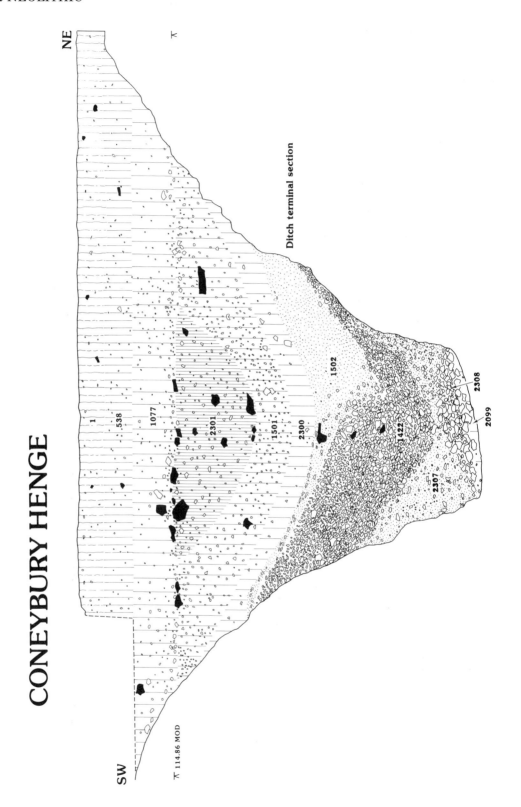

CONEYBURY HENGE

NE

SW

Ditch terminal section

114.86 MOD

1

538

1077

2301

1501

2300

1502

2308

2099

1422

2307

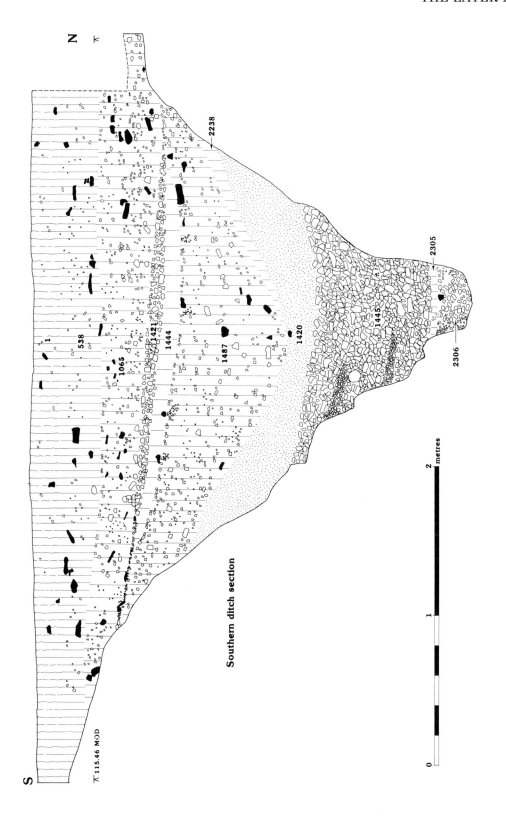

N

2238

2305

2306

1445

1420

1

538

1421

1444

1065

1487

Southern ditch section

115.46 MOD

S

metres

2

1

0

74 Comparative ditch sections from Coneybury Henge.

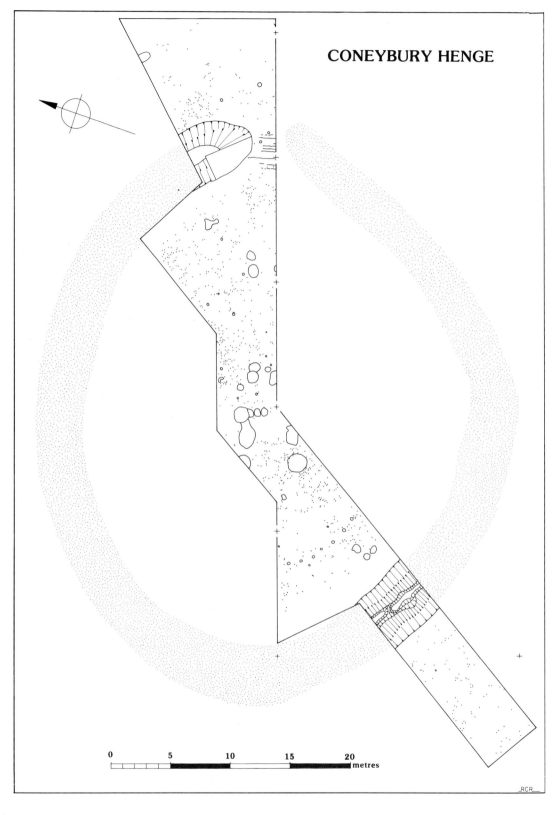

CONEYBURY HENGE

0   5   10   15   20
metres

RCR

76 *Coneybury Henge in the Late Neolithic. Environmental evidence from the excavation suggests that the henge was built in a relatively small woodland clearing (Jane Brayne).*

77 *Location map of Durrington Walls and Woodhenge.*

Perhaps the most unusual feature of the interior was the large number of stake-holes, over 700 in total, revealed by careful excavation and cleaning of the surface of the hard chalk bedrock. The stake-holes, usually about 6 or 7cm ($2\frac{1}{2}$ or 3 in.) in diameter, were apparently created by banging sharpened stakes into the chalk. It is almost impossible to prove whether or not they are associated with the prehistoric activity within the henge, but many showed a strong relationship to both the enclosure as a whole and to internal features, the date of which is beyond doubt.

Coneybury is the smallest, and the least obvious henge within the Stonehenge

75 *Plan of Coneybury Henge.*

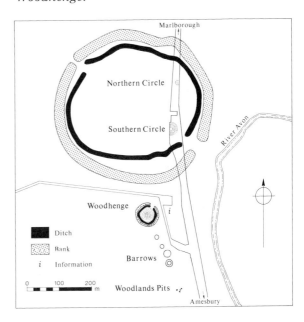

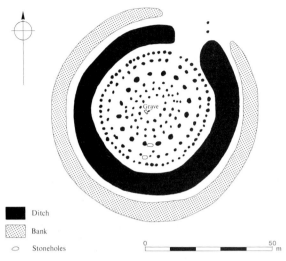

Ditch

Bank

Stoneholes

0   50
m

78 *Plan of Woodhenge as revealed by Cunnington's excavation.*

Environs, but it does share many characteristics with Stonehenge itself. Both have early dates for their initial construction, and both, from environmental data recovered from their ditches, appear to have been rapidly abandoned and overgrown after a brief initial period of use. The similarity in ceramic association is particularly striking, as both have been shown to contain Grooved Ware, but in quantities which appear minuscule when compared to the assemblages from both Woodhenge and, more specifically and strikingly, Durrington Walls. These two riverside henges (**77**) form the most conspicuous single focus of later Neolithic activity within the Stonehenge area, and are

set within a cluster of unusual pits of similar date.

Woodhenge

Woodhenge lies on the crest of a ridge overlooking a bend in the River Avon about 3 km (2 miles) to the north-east of Stonehenge. In the early years of the nineteenth century sufficient traces were recognizable on the ground for the site to be shown on Colt Hoare's map of the Stonehenge Environs, and described as the remains of a large 'druid barrow', the term then used to describe a disc barrow. In the early part of the twentieth century little remained visible at ground level as the site was under cultivation, but aerial photographs taken in 1925 by Squadron-Leader G.S.M. Insall showed the true nature of the site. Within the interior of a roughly circular enclosure, defined by a ditch and an external bank, several concentric rings of darker spots suggested pits cut into the underlying chalk. The similarity between the ground plan of Stonehenge and this newly discovered site, and the possibility that these holes might have held long-vanished upright timbers prompted the name Woodhenge.

Excavations carried out by Maud Cunnington shortly after this discovery confirmed the initial interpretation. Conforming with the

79 *Woodhenge today, the position of the wooden posts revealed by excavation marked with concrete bollards of appropriate diameter. This approach to presentation has its critics but does enable the symmetry of the layout to be appreciated at ground level.*

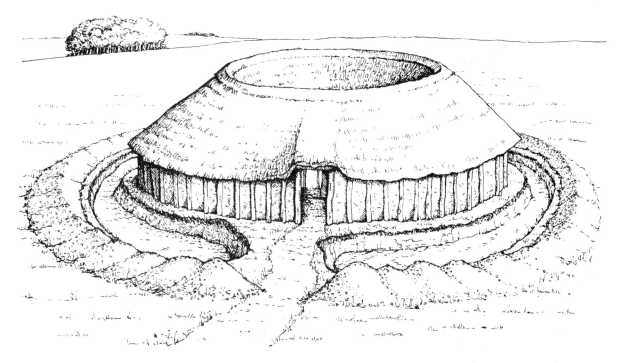

80 *Woodhenge as a roofed building. The plan (see 78) may represent the remains of a structure of this type, a building with an open central area (Jane Brayne).*

pattern of true henges, the shallow and much-damaged bank at Woodhenge was shown to lie on the exterior of the broad, flat-bottomed ditch. A single entrance, marked by post-holes, faced north-east. The holes which had appeared on the aerial photographs were shown to be the settings for six concentric arrangements of timber uprights, not quite circular in shape. An accurate ground plan of Woodhenge (**78**) shows clearly both the variation in the size of the individual timbers, and the consistency within each of the concentric settings. The majority of the posts were sufficiently small to be simply dropped into straight-sided post-holes, with the exception of the second and third settings in, where the size of the posts necessitated ramped post-holes. The variation in post size is reflected accurately in the current presentation at Woodhenge, where the positions of the individual posts are marked by concrete bollards of an appropriate diameter (**79**). A flint cairn near the centre of the enclosure now marks the position of a grave, within which lay the skeleton of a child aged about

three, its skull split. From the evidence which has survived from over four millennia, it is impossible to say whether this injury was the cause of death, or whether the skull of a dead child was split as part of a funerary rite. The possibility that the body of this child represents a human sacrifice, perhaps a foundation or dedicatory burial, cannot be ignored.

Unlike Stonehenge, where the enduring stones have preserved the complex structures through the millennia, nothing survives of Woodhenge but a ground plan. In consequence, any discussions of its original appearance are speculative. The name Woodhenge, singularly inappropriate when the origin of that of Stonehenge is considered, carries with it implications of a similar type of structure where uprights carry horizontal jointed lintels. This may have been the case, and if so then the structures at Woodhenge could have provided the inspiration for the later examples at Stonehenge. From the evidence of the ground plan, Woodhenge has been reconstructed, at least on paper, in a variety of forms. Most popularly it appears as a roofed building (**80**) or more simply as an arrangement of free-standing posts, plain or carved, short or tall. All are guesses, some more inspired than others, but whatever its appearance, the construction of Woodhenge appears to demonstrate the

81 *Viewed from Woodhenge, the scale of Durrington Walls henge monument is difficult to appreciate. Beyond the road embankment lies the massive curving ditch and external bank which marks the eastern side of the enclosure. Within its circuit the construction of the road revealed two huge timber circles (82) and geophysical survey suggests more structures of a similar scale exist elsewhere within the henge.*

development of an increasingly complex ideology. This can be identified not only in the richness and unusual nature of the artefacts recovered by excavation, but in the very formal and structured way in which they were deposited. Flint tools, animal bones and the elaborately decorated Grooved Ware pottery; the pattern of distribution of each type of artefact is distinct and points to a formalized use of the space enclosed by the ditch and bank and perhaps more tightly defined by the circular post structures. The exact nature of the ceremonial activities cannot be determined, but the alignment of the enclosure entrance, shared with those of both Stonehenge and Coneybury, indicates a consistent concern with the solstice

at both summer and winter.

Several aspects of Woodhenge suggest that its construction and short but intensive period of use may represent the final display of a declining ritual authority, perhaps best regarded as a Neolithic priesthood. The great henge enclosure of Durrington Walls, immediately north of Woodhenge, provides the most graphic evidence of the achievements of this authority, those with the ability to conceive, construct and maintain sites on a truly monumental scale.

Durrington Walls

Durrington Walls, despite its huge size, comparable to that of Avebury, is a difficult monument to appreciate. This is due primarily to its scale of construction, unexpected in this situation, and also to its position, straddling a shallow coombe running down to the broad floodplain of the River Avon (**81**). The effects of centuries of cultivation have also helped to disguise the outline of the enclosure and have smoothed the contours of the earthworks. The roughly circular enclosure, over 470m (1500 ft) in diameter, has two entrances, one pointing down to the river, the other directly opposite. The scale of the earthwork is huge, the bank about 30m

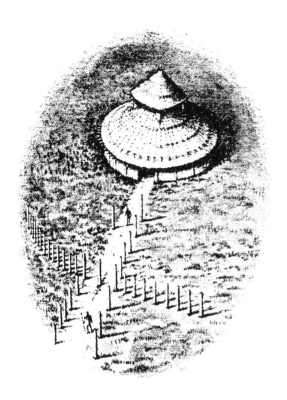

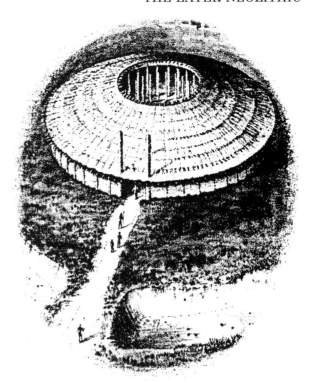

82 *Reconstructions of the timber circles within the henge monument of Durrington Walls (English Heritage).*

(100 ft) wide at its base and now 5m (16½ ft) high at its most undisturbed point. Lying immediately inside this is the ditch, shown by excavation to be 6m (19½ ft) deep and nearly 13m (42 ft) wide at the top. Together the circuit of bank and ditch represent a massive investment in labour and an impressive monument to prehistoric social cohesion. Some insight into the reasons for such a scale of construction was gained from excavations carried out between 1966 and 1968 in advance of a road improvement scheme. The excavations, very typical of the large-scale 'rescue' response of that era, examined not only the enclosure ditch and bank, but also a north-south swathe through the interior. In the area which now lies beneath the road embankment, sealed beneath layers of soil washed down the slope by centuries of ploughing, lay the remains of two circular timber structures (see 77), structures which more recent geophysical survey has suggested are only part of a complex of activity extending over the whole interior of the site.

The larger and more complex of the structures revealed by excavation, the Southern Circle, lay just inside the eastern entrance. In its original form it consisted of four nearly concentric circles of slender posts, with a maximum diameter of 23m (75 ft), fronted on the south-east by a facade of closely-set posts. It appears that this structure was allowed to decay and was then replaced by a more substantial construction. This consisted of six nearly concentric rings of posts, not only much larger than those of the original structure, but now set into ramped post-holes.

Just over 120m (400 ft) to the north of the circle described above lay the Northern Circle, a much simpler structure consisting of a double circle of uprights with an overall diameter of about 14.5m (47 ft). This building was apparently approached from the south by an avenue of spaced posts which pass through a curved facade or fence line.

The similarity between the Southern Circle and Woodhenge has led to suggestions of a comparable original appearance (82). A common element is the thatched building with a central open space, a light-well to illuminate elaborate ceremonies, or simply the everyday activities for which these buildings were constructed. Durrington Walls was originally interpreted by its excavators as having been built for communal or ceremonial purposes and the massive internal structures were regarded as being unlikely to be purely domestic. Additional support for this idea appeared to come from the considerable quantities of debris associated with both these structures and with other formal areas of deposition. Large quantities of animal bone, Grooved Ware pottery and fine flint tools were seen as possible offerings, placed at the base of the timber posts within the ceremonial circles (83).

Although the large-scale and extremely well-defined activity at Durrington Walls was interpreted as resulting from ceremonial practices, the excavation of the site was seen as being a starting point in the search for the elusive settlements of the later Neolithic period. Several years later one of the excavators, Dr Wainwright, offered an alternative interpretation, in which the size of enclosures such as Durrington Walls, together with the elements

originally interpreted as ceremonial, are allocated a more secular function. Both seem perfectly reasonable explanations of the evidence, although there are apparently valid arguments against each. The purely ceremonial interpretation denies the possibility that society could be sufficiently organized and close-knit to produce and maintain a complex nucleated settlement on such a scale. Alternatively, the entirely domestic interpretation fails to explain both the absence of Woodhenge/Durrington type timber structures beyond the confines of such enclosures, and also the huge contrast between the quantity and status of artefacts from sites such as Durrington Walls and from contemporary sites of a clearly non-ceremonial type. In a

83 Highly decorated Grooved Ware pottery may have been placed with other offerings in the timber circles at Durrington Walls (Jane Brayne).

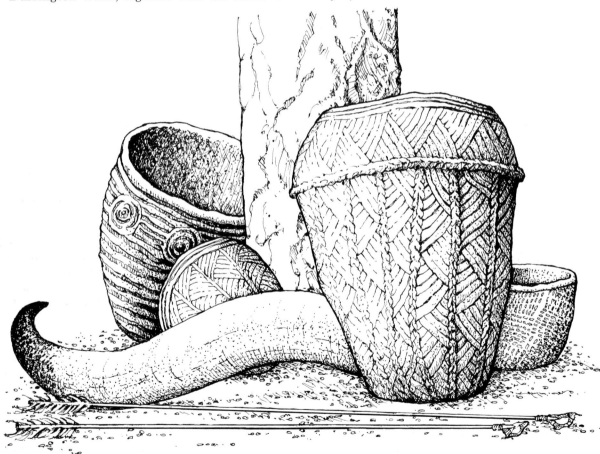

84 *Decorated Neolithic chalk plaques discovered in 1968 in a pit close to the King Barrow Ridge (Elizabeth James).*

form of uneasy compromise, Durrington Walls may best be interpreted in a way which accomodates both concepts, as an area of rigidly defined settlement activity, constructed and used in a manner embodying equally rigid ideological codes. The contrast provided by this structured and highly recognizable activity, and the extensive but ephemeral activity represented beyond the confines of the enclosure, suggests more than simple status divisions operating within later Neolithic society.

The Durrington Zone

Whatever the interpretation of Woodhenge and Durrington Walls, the later Neolithic ceremonial focus within the Stonehenge area seems to be concentrated in the zone stretching from the King Barrow Ridge eastwards to the River Avon. This 'Durrington Zone' appears to represent a shift of emphasis away from the areas within which lie the majority of the identifiable focal monuments of the earlier Neolithic, including the Cursus and the abandoned first phase of Stonehenge.

Prior to recent survey work the Durrington Zone had also produced the only evidence for later Neolithic activity beyond the group of ceremonial monuments described above. Traces of settlement extending for about 150m (495 ft) south of Woodhenge were located during the excavation of a series of ploughed barrows in the 1920s and slightly further south, a group of pits was located at a later date. The Woodlands pits, named after the house in the garden of which they were found, offer a contrast to the settlement traces nearby, as they do not appear to be domestic in nature. The capping of flint nodules over two of the pits, and their contents, including Grooved Ware, an exceptional range of animal bones, bone needles, marine shells, a fragment of a stone axe from Cornwall (Group vii) and finely-worked flint arrowheads, appear to offer evidence for a type of formal deposition, perhaps ideologically motivated.

Effectively within the same broad zone, the widening of a road, the A303, in 1968 revealed several pits of Neolithic date, including one containing not only sherds of Grooved Ware but also two unusual decorated plaques of chalk (84). With the exception of the plaques, the contents of the pit appear undistinguished and the circumstances under which the finds were deposited do not seem to show any of the elements of formality represented in the Woodlands examples. The evidence from the Durrington Zone cannot be taken to suggest a landscape given over solely to ritual, but one within which ceremonial monuments and activities played a significant role within a wider context of domestic and economic life. Evidence for this context has only recently been provided by the programme of extensive surface collection.

Beyond the henges

Within the wider Stonehenge landscape it can be suggested that Stonehenge Bottom, the major north-south dry valley, may have acted as a conceptual, if not physical, barrier to separate zones of varying activity, emphasis and association.

With two exceptions, a concentration on Wilsford Down and the small quantity of material from Stonehenge itself, the distribution of Grooved Ware pottery, with its associations with such sites as Woodhenge and Durrington Walls, is exclusively within the eastern part of the study area. Concentrations of flint tools of later Neolithic type are again found on the King Barrow Ridge and south onto Coneybury Hill.

Towards what has already been suggested as

a major focus, the area of Durrington Walls and Woodhenge, the distribution of later Neolithic flint tools becomes surprisingly extremely sparse. Scattered arrowheads and other typically later Neolithic tools show no indication either of extensive activity or of more nucleated 'sites' and, immediately adjacent to Woodhenge, the fields are characterized by an almost total absence of worked flint. It can be suggested that many of the later Neolithic activities in this particular area were of an enclosed nature, either physically within ditches and banks of earth, or perhaps more symbolically, as those sealed beneath a layer of flints within the Woodlands pits. The patterns observed here provide a strong contrast with those observed in the western half of the study area.

To the west of Stonehenge Bottom finds from surface collection suggest a number of areas of varying activity, and in some cases, where ploughing has only taken place since the Second World War, fragile pottery of later Neolithic date survives to be collected.

The most identifiable and discrete concentration of flint tools occurs within the arable field immediately to the west of Stonehenge. Here, within an area bounded by the low ridge of Stonehenge Down to the south, and by the line of the modern road to the north, a concentration of transverse arrowheads was recorded, together with fabricators, fragments of stone axes and occasional sherds of Peterborough Ware pottery.

To the north of the Stonehenge Cursus as far north as Durrington Down lies an area of over 50ha (120 acres), within which the evidence from surface collection suggests extensive later Neolithic activity. Within this broadly defined scatter individual focal points can be identified, represented by a variety of artefact combinations, and potentially indicating a wide range of differing functions. Peterborough Ware pottery of a variety of styles occurs in combination with arrowheads, fabricators and scrapers.

To the south-west of Stonehenge, away from the concentration of ceremonial sites with their exotic associations, lies an area given over to more mundane activities. In the shallow coombes beyond Normanton Down in the area of Wilsford Down, both surface collection and excavation have shown extensive traces of industrial activity, flint extraction and working

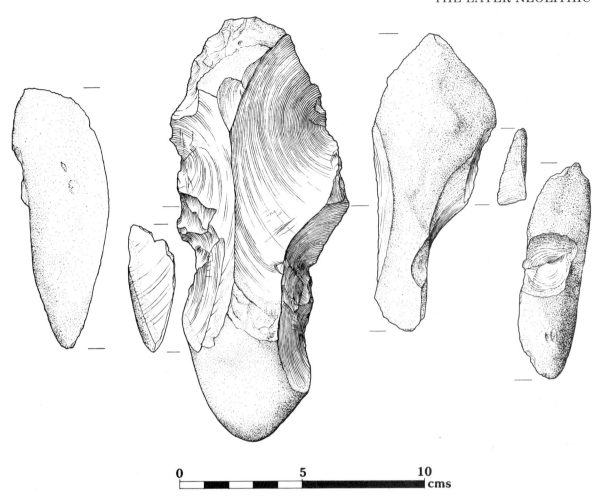

0   5   10
                    cms

85 *The manufacture of a Neolithic flint axe. The roughed-out flint axe, together with the flakes removed in its shaping, were found in 1983 during excavations on Wilsford Down (Julian Cross).*

on a large scale. In the same way, however, that the Durrington Zone should not be seen as exclusively ritual in emphasis, this 'Wilsford Zone' includes domestic activity within a broadly industrial function.

The industrial activity is focused on the dry valley running up towards Wilsford Down from the River Avon at Wilsford-cum-Lake. Seams of good quality flint nodules outcrop along the sides of this shallow coombe, sufficiently close to the surface to be recovered by grubbing rather than more concerted mining. Once extracted it appears that these nodules were

'tested' for flaws, and discarded if found to be unusable. At some extraction sites the chalky 'cortex', or outer skin of the nodule, was also immediately flaked away to reveal the pure flint inside. The majority of these sites are characterized by scatters of 'cortical' flakes, suggesting that the flint, in the form of rough cores, was taken away for working elsewhere. Small numbers of finished tools point to a domestic component to these sites, however, and excavations on Wilsford Down also provided evidence of some tool manufacture (**85**).

The evidence from surface collection provides hints of later Neolithic activity over wide areas of the Stonehenge landscape. The precise nature of the activity which could have generated the patterns of surface artefacts is open to speculation. The small-scale excavations which have been carried out in order to further investigate this problem have not so far provided

103

any greater insight beyond scatters of pits containing what must be regarded as domestic rubbish. Scatters of flint tools, particularly of such types as scrapers and knives, can be suggested as indicating 'domestic' areas, perhaps permanent settlements which, if investigated extensively, would reveal traces of buildings to go with the clusters of pits located so far. It is possible though, that in contrast with the massive timber buildings found within the henge enclosures, the everyday structures of the Neolithic farmers were so lightly constructed as to leave no recoverable trace.

Despite the shortage of evidence for some aspects of later Neolithic society, recent investigations have allowed an understanding of the ecomomic and subsistence patterns of this period. As this information comes from sites almost exclusively located in the eastern half of the Stonehenge landscape, which are also essentially non-domestic in character, its wider application should be treated with caution. Taken at face value, the pre-enclosure soil at Durrington Walls indicates a grassland environment, perhaps part of an extensive cleared and maintained zone stretching as far west as the King Barrow Ridge. In contrast, and perhaps indicative of the southerly extent of this zone, evidence from the ditch sequence at Coneybury Henge indicates that if the henge was constructed in a cleared area, then the area was likely to have been of small size and seems to have become overgrown in a generation. Although not precisely dated, and potentially only representative of a localized sequence, the evidence for scrub regeneration at Stonehenge provides further evidence that the later Neolithic is not represented solely by increasingly more extensive forest clearance.

Evidence for woodland management is difficult to interpret, although the continuing use of woodland food resources is evident throughout this period (**colour plate 4**). Wild animals, particularly deer, can now be regarded as no more than a supplement to a diet based on domestic animals, with cattle and pig dominant. The pig, an animal suited to roaming within areas of managed woodland, is particularly well represented at Durrington Walls, where it is seen as a source of meat for feasting. Evidence from the Stonehenge area suggests that sheep were very poorly represented throughout the whole of the Neolithic period.

Elsewhere in southern Britain the final stage of the Neolithic is a period that incorporated a wider range of developments than those represented in the Stonehenge area. This period saw the introduction of Beakers, finely-made pots at first decorated with an overall pattern of cord impressions (see **16**) and of the first metalwork initially in the form of copper weapons, albeit in small quantities. It is also clear that round barrows were being constructed in perhaps greater numbers than currently available information suggests. Of these innovations, only the earliest styles of Beakers can consistently be identified within the Stonehenge area. Small numbers of sherds, primarily of 'All-Over-Corded' Beakers, are distributed almost exclusively in the area of Wilsford Down.

Within the Stonehenge landscape there is clearly a major shift in emphasis which marks the transition from the later Neolithic to the earlier Bronze Age. The motivation for this shift, the evidence for which again rests mainly on ceremonial and funerary monuments, could consequently be regarded as purely connected with ideology, but economic factors may have played an equally important part.

In chronological terms, it appears that the construction of the extensive ceremonial and funerary landscape described in the following chapter overlaps with the final phases of identifiable activity at Durrington Walls, Woodhenge and Coneybury. All produced Beaker pottery from high levels in their ditches and in some cases from high within the filling of interior pits. Perhaps one of the most dramatic aspects of the shift which now takes place is the abandonment of the Durrington Zone, demonstrated not only by the disuse of the monuments themselves, but in changing patterns of wider land use.

Around Durrington Walls the long-established pasture now appears to be abandoned and the environmental sequence from Coneybury Henge shows little evidence of the maintenance of the clearing within which the henge was constructed. If the old authority is now declining and an air of dereliction falls over the true henges, then the activities just to the west, on and beyond the King Barrow Ridge provide a remarkable contrast of regeneration and expansion.

8

The earlier Bronze Age

Recent research has demonstrated that the area around Avebury in north Wiltshire represents a Neolithic landscape of increasing complexity, the momentum of which dies down in the succeeding Bronze Age. A marked contrast is provided by the Stonehenge area, where a dramatic shift away from the monuments and broader areas so favoured in the later Neolithic, is followed by the development of a ceremonial and funerary landscape of unparalleled visual impact and splendour.

For reasons that are uncertain, some time around 2000 BC the small and long-abandoned

86 *The New King Barrows in September 1990. Gales in January 1990 almost totally flattened the 200-year-old beech wood in which the barrows lay, exposing the true scale of the massive mounds. Archaeological recording of the damage is now complete and the fallen timber cleared from the barrows.*

87 Part of the Normanton Down barrow group facing north towards Stonehenge. Two magnificent disc barrows lie either side of the track on the left of the photograph. Close to them, still marked by bushes, is Bush Barrow. Compare this view with that engraved by Stukeley in 1723 (see 20) (Mick Aston).

enclosure at Stonehenge was selected for reconstruction and enhancement on a grand scale. As described in chapter 4 the earlier Bronze Age phase at Stonehenge itself is represented by a series of major events involving the remodelling and augmentation of the original, long-abandoned enclosure. These events include the modification of the original entrance to the enclosure and the construction of the first straight stage of the Avenue, together with the start of the building in the interior which sees its final form in the paired circles and horseshoes of both sarsen and bluestone.

Viewed in isolation, the revived Stonehenge is a remarkable individual monument. Its importance as the ceremonial focus of an exten-

sive and highly-structured funerary landscape cannot, however, be over-emphasized.

The barrow cemeteries

The area defined as the Stonehenge Environs could, quite justifiably, be regarded as one huge and densely-populated round barrow cemetery. On currently available evidence, the development of this, one of the greatest concentrations of such monuments anywhere in Britain, started very early in the second millennium BC. The available radiocarbon dates for primary burials in round barrows in the immediate area of Stonehenge (see 6), show a strong correlation with those available for the broad phase of Stonehenge described above.

Despite the overall density of round barrows within the Stonehenge Environs, there has long been an awareness, developed initially during the period of antiquarian study in the early nineteenth century, of a number of discrete barrow clusters. These, often sited conspicuously on ridge tops, have become identified as individual cemeteries. The major examples within the Stonehenge area are the linear cemeteries of the Old and New King Barrows (**86**), the Normanton Down Group (**87**), the Winterbourne Stoke Crossroads Group (see **18** and **colour plate 6**) and the Cursus Group (**88**). More clustered groups lie further south on Wilsford and Lake Downs (see **32**) and to the north on Durrington Down.

The individual cemeteries vary considerably in both their component barrows and in their layout, with Winterbourne Stoke Crossroads exhibiting the greatest variety of barrow types and the strongest visual evidence for sequence and development. Here the massive long barrow provides the focus and alignment for the linear arrangement of round barrows, constructed 1000 years later and initially of large bowl and bell barrows. Bowl barrows (**89**) are simple

88 *The Cursus Barrow group. Part of this group, a line of large bowl and bell barrows are prominently sited on the crest of a low ridge to the north-east of Stonehenge. They lie close to the much earlier Stonehenge Cursus which can be seen on the photograph as parallel ditches and banks beyond the barrows (Mick Aston).*

round mounds usually surrounded by a ditch. Larger examples tend to be earlier in date and quite tiny bowl barrows can often be found within larger cemeteries, giving the appearance of having been tucked in as later additions. Bell barrows, when undamaged, can be distinguished by the flat area, the 'berm' which lies between the inner edge of the ditch and the edge of the mound. While the more massive mounds form the obvious skyline features of many of the Stonehenge barrow cemeteries, subsequent additions in the form of lower 'fancy' barrows can best be appreciated from aerial views. At Winterbourne Stoke Crossroads the full range of such types is represented in the form of disc, saucer and pond barrows. Both disc and saucer barrows have ditches with external banks, enclosing in the case of the disc, one or more small mounds or 'tumps' and, in the saucer, a shallow, gently-sloping mound. The pond barrow, which rarely survives in a recognizable form, consists of a circular depression with a surrounding bank. A clear indication of sequence can be seen at this cemetery where the ditch of a large bell barrow is impinged upon and partly cut away by the construction of a pond barrow.

89 *Bronze Age round barrow types. Bowl barrows are simple round mounds of varying size and often surrounded by a ditch. Bell barrows can be distinguished by the flat area (the 'berm') between mound and ditch. Disc barrows and saucer barrows have ditches with banks outside enclosing, in the case of the disc,* one or more small mounds ('tumps') and, in the saucer, a shallow, gentle mound. Pond barrows consist of a circular depression with a surounding bank. Many unmarked burials may lie between the visible barrows (Jane Brayne).

The survival of round barrows within the Stonehenge Environs is naturally heavily biased in favour of those types which offer some resistance to the effects of cultivation. Pond barrows can easily be filled in, and are then indistinguishable from dew ponds or marl pits; disc and saucer barrows can easily be ploughed over. Fortunately, many of the larger bowl and bell barrows have survived, even within heavily-cultivated areas, where ploughing often reaches up to the edge of the mound. In such cases the distinction between bowl and bell barrows is difficult to see.

As noted by many previous observers, the King Barrows, the Normanton Down group and the Cursus Barrows are carefully positioned on the crests of low ridges to the east, south and north-west of Stonehenge respectively, positions in which the mounds of the more substantial barrows are silhouetted against the skyline. Of these groups, the King Barrows, and to a lesser degree the Cursus Barrows, appear unusual in their failure to develop into true Wessex cemeteries, exemplified by Winterbourne Stoke Crossroads with its complement of 'fancy' barrow forms. The reason for the King Barrows consisting entirely of bowl and bell barrows may relate to their somewhat peripheral position at the easterly edge of the ceremonial/funerary zone centred on Stonehenge. Although these barrows have never been investigated, the only effectively undisturbed group within the Stonehenge Environs, they are potentially of early date in the sequence of round barrow construction. As a group they may also be acting as a boundary, perhaps closing-off from Stonehenge the area formerly of such ideological significance. Recent investigations of holes torn into the mounds of a number of the King Barrows by falling trees have shown that many of the mounds, including some of the extremely large examples are substantially turf-built (**90**). To obtain sufficient turf for the construction of mounds of this size would involve stripping a considerable area. The effect of this would be a form of physical, if not symbolic 'sterilization' of a large part of the King Barrow Ridge. This method of construction does not seem to be consistently represented within any of the other barrow cemeteries in the Stonehenge area.

The topographic relationship between Stonehenge and the barrow cemeteries around it is clearly visible, but less easy to characterize is the concept of a complementary focal area on Wilsford Down, to which the cemeteries of Lake, Normanton Down and Winterbourne Stoke Crossroads appear to be related. Focal to this suggested zone is another unique monument, the Wilsford Down 'North Kite'.

The Wilsford Down 'North Kite'

The 'North Kite' is a large three-sided earthwork enclosure, lying on a north-facing slope of Wilsford Down, immediately adjacent to the Lake barrow group (**91**). In 1928 an aerial photograph of the site was published by O.G.S. Crawford and Alexander Keiller in *Wessex from the Air*. At this time a Romano-British date was suggested and Colt Hoare's description of the enclosure as originally having a fourth side was repeated. Subsequent to this publication much of the enclosure earthwork was levelled by ploughing, with only a short section of the western side surviving intact beyond the edge of the Lake Wood.

In 1958 Ernest Greenfield made a number of exploratory cuttings through both the levelled and the surviving areas of the enclosure. The suggested fourth side was not located but one cutting produced pottery of both later Neolithic and earlier Bronze Age date from beneath the bank. This revision of the date suggested by Crawford and Keiller was confirmed by observations made by the Royal Commission on the Historic Monuments of England. Within Lake Wood, they noted that some of the round barrows of the Lake cemetery, specifically disc barrow Wilsford 45b, overlie the western side of the enclosure. This too suggests a construction date in the earlier Bronze Age and a further excavation in 1983, close to one of Greenfield's cuttings, produced even more conclusive dating evidence. Here, as well as pottery of types similar to those found by Greenfield, including Grooved Ware and Peterborough Ware, sherds of freshly broken Beaker were found on the old ground surface sealed by the chalk bank (**92**).

This buried land surface also contained three freshly-broken pieces of spotted dolerite (bluestone), providing a link with the reconstructions being carried out beyond the crest of Normanton Down at Stonehenge.

Burial

The earlier Bronze Age provides a considerable contrast to the later Neolithic period, when

90 *The structure of the mound of barrow Amesbury G 32 within the New King Barrows exposed by the roots of a fallen tress in January 1990. The dark turf core and subsequent white chalk capping of the mound are clearly visible.*

effort was expended on the construction of communal monuments, and the burials of either groups or individuals appear to be almost totally absent. This may be at least partly due to a lack of recognition of later Neolithic round barrows, although the contrast appears too great to ignore. From around 2000 BC the dead, or at least the powerful dead, are conspicuous

under round barrows, their grave goods proclaiming a new wealth, a new form of authority. Ideological power may have constructed and briefly sustained Durrington Walls and Woodhenge, but the power of prestige items probably lay behind the reconstruction of Stonehenge.

The energetic campaigns of Colt Hoare and Cunnington in the early years of the nineteenth century have been briefly described in chapter 3. The results, published in *Ancient Wiltshire* provide detailed descriptions of the barrows and their contents, fortunately linked to Philip

91 *Plan of the Wilsford Down North Kite.*

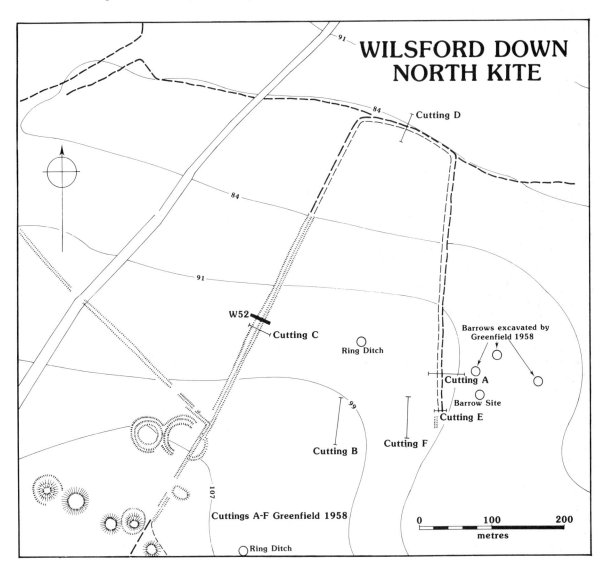

92 Excavation of the bank of the North Kite in 1983. The thin dark line beneath the chalk bank is the Bronze Age land surface, a well-developed grassland turf buried in about 1700 BC.

Crocker's extraordinarily accurate maps. This level of detail, combined with the magnificent collection of artefacts now housed in Devizes Museum, provide much of the basis for our understanding of the funerary practices and chronology of this period around Stonehenge.

Thorough as these investigators were for their time, they had no interest in the human remains contained within the barrows that they so eagerly explored. The nature of the burial rite was usually noted, together with occasional references to stature or unusually solid bones, but for positive information it is necessary to turn to more recent excavations, often of barrows previously investigated.

A general scheme of association between barrow type, burial rite and grave goods can be suggested, but the patterns revealed by both antiquarian and more recent excavations often suggest a greater complexity. The various types of barrows have already been described, and some idea of sequence introduced. In terms of burial rite, both inhumation, usually in a crouched position (see **19**), but occasionally extended, was practised alongside cremation. There seems to be no chronological distinction between these two rites, although when found together within the same grave, the inhumation always appears to be in a primary position. This introduces the possibility of social status, of differing burial rites for people of different sex, age or rank. Family custom or even individual preference, exercised in current society, could equally play a part in the decision of which rite to choose. Where available for study, inhumations and, less easily, cremations, can be assessed for age and sex, but status depends on the survival of grave goods and on our interpretation of their implied meaning.

A range of pottery types can be identified from the Bronze Age barrow burials amongst the Stonehenge cemeteries. Beakers, the finely-potted, uniformly red vessels, often highly-decorated with either cord or toothed-comb impressions belong to the earliest part of the Bronze Age. Food vessels and collared urns (**93**) follow in an overlapping sequence which may

again have much to do with individual preference.

Even within the great catalogue of barrow finds from Colt Hoare's Stonehenge Environs, the spectacular contents of a few barrows stand out as evidence of a new individual wealth and power. Alongside the decorated pottery and the weapons of bronze appear beads of shale, jet and glass, and ornaments of gold. Perhaps the most important amongst these Early Bronze Age 'Wessex' graves, which together led to the identification of the so-called 'Wessex Culture', was discovered within the Normanton Down

93 Bronze Age pottery styles (after Gibson).

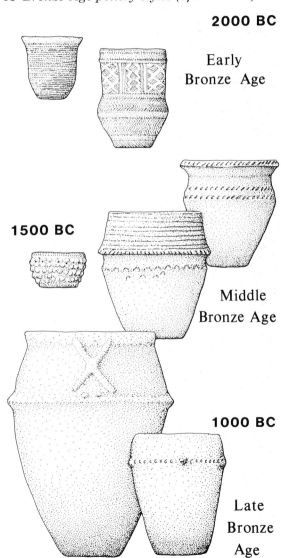

2000 BC

Early Bronze Age

1500 BC

Middle Bronze Age

1000 BC

Late Bronze Age

Barrow cemetery. William Stukeley had engraved the Bush Barrow in the early eighteenth century (94) showing it crowned with a sheep fold, and in September 1808, at the second excavation attempt, William Cunnington and his labourers discovered the burial:

On reaching the floor of the barrow we discovered the skeleton of a stout and tall man lying from south to north: the extreme length of his thigh bone was 20 inches. About 18 inches south of the head, we found several brass rivets intermixed with wood, and some thin bits of brass nearly decomposed. These articles covered a space of 12 inches or more; it is probable, therefore, that they were the mouldered remains of a shield. Near the shoulders lay the fine celt, the lower end of which owes its great preservation to having been originally inserted within a handle of wood. Near the right arm was a large dagger of brass, and a spear-head of the same metal, full thirteen inches long, and the largest that we have ever found. These were accompanied by a curious article of gold, which I concieve had originally decorated the case of the dagger. The handle of wood belonging to this instrument exceeds anything that we have yet seen, both in design and execution, and could not be surpassed (if indeed equalled) by the most able workman of modern times.

By the annexed engraving [95] you will immediately recognise the British zigzag, which was formed with a labour and exactness almost unaccountable, by thousands of gold rivets, smaller than the smallest pin. The head of the handle, though exhibiting no variety of pattern, was also formed by the same kind of studding. So very minute, indeed, were these pins, that our labourers had thrown out thousands of them with their shovel, and scattered them in every direction, before, with the necessary aid of a magnifying glass, we could discover what they were; but fortunately enough remained attached to the wood to enable us to develop the pattern. Beneath the fingers of the right hand lay a lance-head of brass, but so corroded that it broke to pieces on moving. Immediately over the breast of the skeleton was a large plate of gold [**colour plate 12**], in the form of a lozenge, and measuring 7 inches by 6. It was fixed to a thin piece of wood, over the edges of which the gold was lapped: it is perforated at top and bottom, for the purpose, probably, of fastening it to the dress as a breast-plate.

94 *The Bush Barrow looking towards Stonehenge engraved by William Stukeley in 1723. The hurdle structure on the summit of the barrow is a temporary sheep penning.*

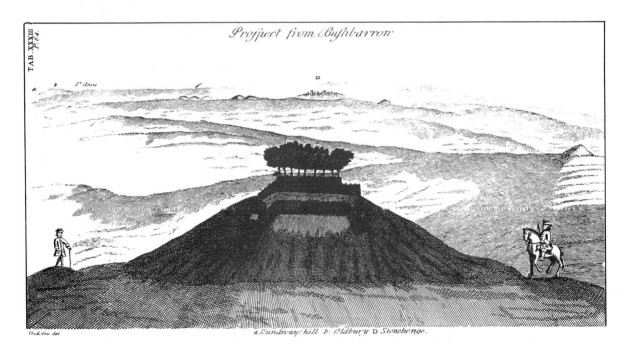

Prospect from Bushbarrow

a. Rundway hill b. Oldbury D. Stonehenge.

95 *Engraving of the Bush Barrow dagger handle from* Ancient Wiltshire. *The 'British zigzag' described by Colt Hoare is clearly visible, executed in tiny gold pins, a few of which are shown below the handle to give some idea of scale.*

The even surface of this noble ornament is relieved by indented lines, checques, and zigzags, following the shape of the outline, and forming lozenge within lozenge, diminishing gradually towards the centre. We next discovered, on the right side of the skeleton, a very curious perforated stone, some wrought articles of bone, many small rings of the same material, and another article of gold. The stone is made out of a fossil mass of *tubularia*, and polished; rather of an egg form, or, as a farmer who was present observed, resembling the top of a gimlet. It had a wooden handle, which was fixed into the perforation in the centre, and encircled by a neat ornament of brass, part of which still adheres to the stone. As this stone bears no marks of wear or attrition, I can hardly consider it to have been used as a domestic implement, and from the circumstances of its being composed of a mass of sea-worms, or little serpents, I think that we may not be too fanciful in considering it an article of consequence.

With this unusual departure from his normally factual tone (*Ancient Wiltshire* starts with the declaration 'We speak from facts not theory'), Colt Hoare completes his description of one of the most remarkable graves in British prehistory. The description of a 'stout and tall man', the weapons of bronze (described as brass), the

possible shield, the gold objects and the curious stone which together with the bone rings can be interpreted as a sceptre, all suggest a person of near regal status. Perhaps we are looking into the burial of the person who revived Stonehenge, the architect, the sponsor, buried in his finery overlooking his lasting monument (**colour plate 13**).

Evidence for settlement

The monuments described above, Stonehenge, the North Kite and the barrows, either individually or in cemeteries, would certainly have exerted local or more widespread constraints on activities such as settlement or cultivation. The King Barrows have already been suggested as performing a boundary function, and other

96 *Bronze Age flint tool types (Julian Cross).*

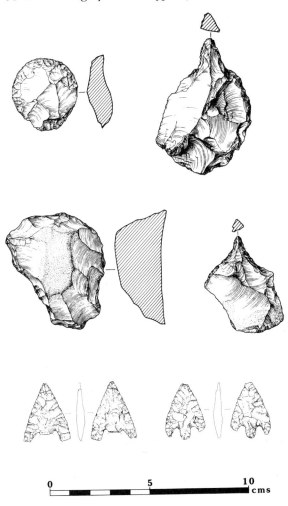

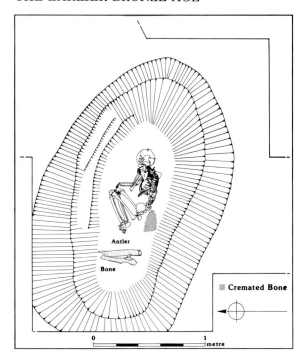

97 The burial of an Early Bronze Age child from a round barrow on Durrington Down.

this date, amongst which for the first time sheep and goats appear in significant numbers.

For the earlier Bronze Age the evidence from

98 *Antler 'toy' found within the grave of the Bronze Age child from a round barrow on Durrington Down (Miranda Schofield).*

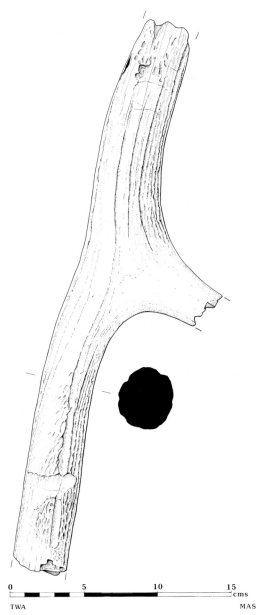

linear barrow cemeteries may have functioned in a similar way. Beyond these monuments the evidence for settlement is still sparse, as is the direct evidence for land-use.

At Stonehenge, perhaps not surprisingly, environmental evidence indicates the localized creation and maintenance of open grassland. It is tempting to extend this pattern as far as the assumedly-visible barrow cemeteries, the King Barrows, Normanton Down and the Cursus Barrows, and consequently to suggest a zone of grassland surrounding Stonehenge. It is possible that, within such an area, taboos may have operated to prevent either settlement or cultivation, in a form of 'ritual exclusion zone'. The extent of such a zone is, however, unproven, as is any firm indication of extensive and more formalized arable cultivation during the earlier Bronze Age. All the evidence though, whether inferred from the many descriptions of soil profiles beneath round barrows, or from the analysis of land snails, consistently indicates extensive areas of maintained grassland within the western half of the area (**colour plate 5**). This is corroborated by the animal bones recovered from deposits of

116

surface collection differs considerably from that available for the Neolithic period. The newly-introduced barbed-and-tanged flint arrowheads are extremely rare surface finds, in contrast to the considerable quantities found casually in the past in other chalkland areas of southern England. The identification of an earlier Bronze Age component within the huge quantities of surface collection flint artefacts consequently has to rely on a small number of datable tool types. These include borers (also known as piercers), 'tool kits' (a borer and a scraper on the same flake), together with specific types of scraper, particularly the small, finely made 'thumbnail' type (96). Pottery of this period which appears to be increasingly robust and capable of surviving the effects of cultivation, provides important dating evidence.

Although the information for this period shows a similar broad emphasis on those areas which demonstrated extensive later Neolithic activity, discrete clusters of artefacts can for the first time be identified. Three locations stand out: an area immediately south of Winterbourne Stoke Crossroads, another within the arable fields to the west of Stonehenge, and the third adjacent to Fargo Wood to the north of the Stonehenge Cursus. In all these cases surface collection revealed a combination of domestic pottery and of identifiable earlier Bronze Age flint tools.

Not all the pottery from surface collection can be considered as settlement debris however, as some, rarely found outside a funerary context, may represent ploughed-out burials, not necessarily buried originally beneath barrow mounds.

Beyond this small number of possible settlement sites, more scattered patterns of pottery and flint represent a wide range of activities. Within an open grassland landscape arable cultivation may be spreading, resulting in the beginnings of more formal field systems. Indeed some of the less comprehensible patterns of pottery distribution may be showing evidence for the practice of manuring fields, an activity which spreads domestic debris along with the manure, at times some distance away from the settlement site. A further indication of the beginnings of more formal cultivation may be provided by isolated small barrows on Durrington Down to the north of the Cursus. Excavation of the heavily-ploughed remains of Durrington G7, built in around 2000 BC, showed that the barrow originally consisted of a cairn constructed of flint nodules. This form of construction is unusual in the Stonehenge area and may suggest that the construction of a funerary cairn was combined with field clearance. This particular barrow appears to form the focus for a field boundary which, rather than being a later landscape feature (the traditional view) may be contemporary with the barrow. The dating evidence for this barrow was provided by the primary burial, that of a young child, buried in an unusually large and deep grave (97). A deposit of cremated bones was also placed in the grave, together with an unusual object, a length of antler with curiously smoothed patches on its surface (98). It is difficult to suggest a function for such an object, but perhaps we are seeing a favourite toy buried with a child not yet ready for the daggers, beads or beakers of more adult life.

The evidence from the area to the north of Stonehenge, although slight, does point to the origins of arable cultivation in the earlier Bronze Age. In common with much of Britain both individual buildings and settlements of the earlier Bronze Age have proved elusive although the patterns of settlement and land-use which can be identified in the later Bronze Age must surely have had much earlier origins.

9

The later Bronze Age

The earlier part of the Bronze Age discussed in the preceding chapter (broadly speaking the first half of the second millennium BC) saw the most dramatic changes in both Stonehenge and in its surrounding landscape. These centuries saw construction involving the investment of hundreds of thousands of hours of labour, and ended with the relatively small-scale modifications at Stonehenge itself. These final phases, the digging of the 'Y' and 'Z' holes, and the possibly piecemeal extension of the Avenue, complete a unique longevity and it is remarkable that Stonehenge, representing an archaic monumental tradition, should continue to be maintained over such a long period of time. As the Bronze Age progressed, the ideological emphasis moves further towards the funerary, although within the area surrounding Stonehenge there is surprisingly little evidence for a parallel development of the funerary landscape. It appears that the addition of fancy barrows of Wessex form to many of the Early Bronze Age cemeteries may represent the final easily identifiable phase of extension. As already noted, however, the small bowl barrows which can be seen in peripheral positions at some barrow cemeteries, may be of later Bronze Age (Deverel-Rimbury) date.

Less obvious to assess, both from surface observation and from the records of past excavation, in which the emphasis lay in the burial record of the barrow mound itself, is the potential for secondary burials. The practice of inserting burials either into or around existing barrows is well-attested, in some cases a single mound acting as the focus for over 100 secondary burials. There is little evidence for this in the immediate area of Stonehenge however, the nearest example being the 18 cremations

recovered from the ditch of barrow Shrewton 5a, approximately 4km (2½ miles) to the north-west of Stonehenge. A more recently excavated barrow, Durrington G7, described in chapter 8, produced considerable evidence for a wide variety of secondary funerary activities including cremations and a secondary crouched inhumation buried in a flint-capped pit. It is likely that the excavation of entire barrows, and perhaps more importantly the areas between barrows, would produce a good deal more evidence for secondary burial. In the absence of such evidence it is difficult to assess the relationship of the final Stonehenge with its surrounding funerary landscape.

The agricultural landscape

What can be discussed with more confidence is the relationship of Stonehenge to a rapidly developing agricultural landscape. The framework of this, even when effectively destroyed by ploughing, can still be recovered from aerial photographs. The patterns of 'Celtic' fields, boundaries and to a certain extent settlements, have been suggested as having their origins within the earlier part of the Bronze Age. In some cases settlement shows evidence, if not of strict continuity, then of the maintenance of broadly preferred locations.

In the later Bronze Age, for the first time, the patterns of surface artefacts can be related to an extensive framework of essentially domestic activity. The identification of flint tools belonging to this period does cause considerable problems however. Metal is now more widely available and is used for tools, in many cases replacing the flint tools of the earlier Bronze Age when bronze was reserved for prestige items such as weapons. In the absence

99 *Preparing grain on a saddle quern (Jane Brayne).*

of specific types of flint tool, and an evident decline in the ability to work flint, it is tempting to fall back on more roughly made, or unspecific tools. Unfortunately these may well date to earlier periods and simply reflect the need for rapidly produced tools to meet the requirements of an immediate task.

Pottery, of both Deverel-Rimbury and Late Bronze Age types, appears to survive well, as do stone saddle querns used for grinding grain (**99**). These artefacts provide positive evidence for the intensification of cereal production, confirmation of which can be seen in the patterns of fields which now develop, particularly within the western half of the area.

Field boundaries of any period can be defined in a number of ways: with ditches, banks, fences, hedges or simply by laying out the stones and other debris from clearance prior to cultivation. Once defined, a field boundary, particularly one which runs across a slope, will

arrest downslope soil movement, caused by the action of water and gravity on loosened soil. This results on the gradual creation of a 'positive lynchet' and downslope soil movement will gradually erode away to create a 'negative lynchet'. The degree of slope, combined with the depth and nature of soil and the type and duration of cultivation will all affect the eventual appearance of the composite lynchet. Within the Stonehenge area, a number of discrete blocks of fields can be identified, and whereas some, such as those on Rox Hill, incorporate quite substantial lynchets on the slopes of the hill, the individual fields of the majority of the other blocks, lying on more gentle slopes, are very weakly defined.

Two of these field systems, on Rox Hill and south of Winterbourne Stoke Crossroads, are linked by a boundary earthwork, a simple ditch and bank running for over 3km (2 miles) across the undulating downland. Such earthworks, which become common within Wessex as a whole at this period, appear to mark the beginnings of defined territories and may suggest that land shortage is becoming a very real problem in some areas.

Although some linear ditches were clearly for territorial division, some more insubstantial examples were perhaps more likely intended for the control of livestock. A complex of such ditches (referred to in the past as 'ranch boundaries') lies in the Wilsford Down area, where the excavation of a unique site in the early 1960s has provided considerable insight into the Middle Bronze Age land-use of the immediate area.

The Wilsford Shaft

The Wilsford Shaft was discovered in 1960 during the course of the excavation of what was presumed to be a pond barrow. Below the shallow depression which defined the pond lay a shaft 1.8m (6ft) in diameter and over 30m (100ft) in depth (**100**). At the bottom of the shaft waterlogging had preserved a remarkable collection of artefacts including fragments of cord and of wooden buckets (**101**) together with a range of environmental data not normally found on the chalklands of Wessex. This feature can be interpreted in two ways, a dilemma very honestly aired in the publication of the excavation report. Paul Ashbee, one of the original excavators, sees it as a shaft providing symbolic access to the underworld and thus

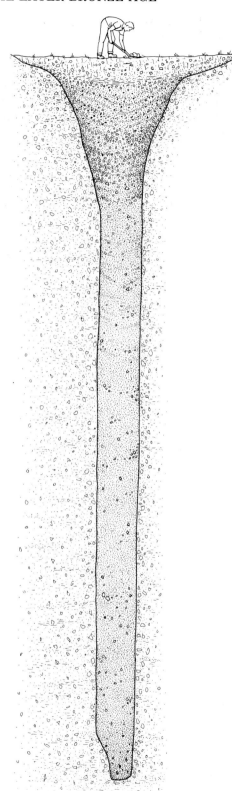

100 *The Wilsford Shaft: a ritual entrance to the underworld or a prehistoric well? (Linda Coleman).*

embodying great ideological significance. Parallels, often of a later (Iron Age or Roman) date, within England and Europe frequently contain offerings, in contrast to what appears to be the accidental accumulation at the base of the Wilsford Shaft. The alternative, proposed by Martin Bell, who oversaw the co-ordination of environmental information, is to interpret it as a well. Large numbers of grazing animals were present in the area, there was possibly a barn storing fodder close by, and at the bottom were the buckets and rope. In the absence of evidence for a nearby settlement the primary function of the shaft is suggested as being to water stock.

The closest known Bronze Age settlement to the shaft, potentially of a slightly later date, was located in 1967 during widening of the A303 road immediately adjacent to the Winterbourne Stoke barrow cemetery. Within an extensive field system, and close to the linear earthwork already noted, settlement traces included the plans of three circular post-built houses (**102**) along with pits, additional post-holes and other features. The settlement clearly extends south of the present road where it has been defined by a scatter of pottery of similar date to that recovered during the excavation.

A further clearly defined area of fields, here too integrated with a settlement area, lies to the north of the Stonehenge Cursus, immediately to the east of Fargo Wood. The settlement area was originally located by surface collection as a dense scatter of pottery, burnt flint and stone and quern fragments. The extent of the scatter suggests a small farmstead, a cluster of houses together with outbuildings for animals, set within its arable fields and pasture (**103** and **colour plate 11**). Evidence from small-scale sample excavation included an almost equal balance of cattle and sheep/goat bones, an indication of a classic mixed farming assemblage.

The reconstruction shown in colour plate 11 is based on archaeological data from a variety of sources. The perspective view looks towards Stonehenge, shown within a large expanse of grassland at the periphery of which are settlements within fields. The closest Late

101 *A Bronze Age bucket from the Wilsford Shaft (Linda Coleman).*

Bronze Age settlement is shown in the position defined by surface collection. The positions of the majority of the fields are as indicated by aerial photographs, although the evidence to suggest that cultivation had extended to include the interior of the long obsolete Cursus was recovered during excavation of this monument. The single barrow close to the clump of trees immediately beyond the edge of the fields

102 *Plan of Bronze Age round houses at Winterbourne Stoke Crossroads.*

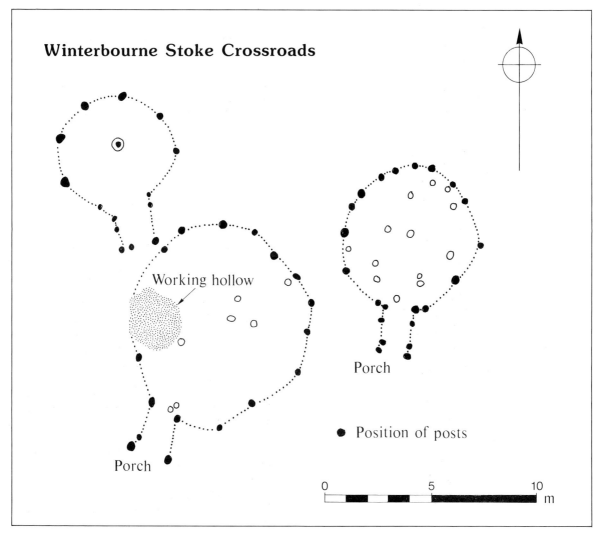

Winterbourne Stoke Crossroads

Working hollow

Porch

Porch

● Position of posts

0   5   10
m

103 *A Bronze Age settlement (Jane Brayne).*

can now only be seen on aerial photographs, but may mark the cemetery for the settlement.

The Durrington 'Egg'
The remaining element of the settlement evidence for the later Bronze Age, and one for which a more pastoral emphasis has been proposed, lies close to the River Avon, immediately south of Woodhenge. The Durrington 'Egg' is

a small enclosure of middle or later Bronze Age date, and was excavated by Maude Cunnington in the early 1920s. The general absence of artefacts from these excavations led to the suggestion that it was for stock rather than for human habitation. Post-holes were recorded within the interior, however, indicating the possible presence of a building, and consequently the original interpretation may not be correct. Economic evidence from the enclosure included charred grains of barley, indicating some involvement in cereal cultivation although the surrounding area appears to be devoid of identifiable 'Celtic' fields.

The later Bronze Age landscape in the Stonehenge area appears to demonstrate a considerable degree of stability, the evidence for which can be seen in the established areas of cultivation and in the continuity of settlement location from the earlier Bronze Age onwards.

The area cannot be considered as marginal in any way, although the thin soils would have had a limited productive capacity without periods of fallow and the application of manure to enhance fertility. It is difficult therefore to suggest the cause, if environmental, for the consistent lack of evidence for settlement from the subsequent Iron Age.

10

The final prehistoric and the historic periods

Throughout the Neolithic and Bronze Age periods the Stonehenge landscape provides clear evidence of many of the environmental and economic trends which also occur elsewhere in southern Britain. Around Stonehenge though, these trends are played out against a background of increasing ideological, political and social complexity. This appears to reach a peak in the earlier Bronze Age with the formality of the ceremonial and funerary landscape centred on the newly revitalized Stonehenge. Subsequent developments, involving the maintenance of what was by then an archaic monument, suggest a degree of conservatism, perhaps linked to the declining economic supremacy of the Wessex chalklands.

By the later Bronze Age this suggested conservatism results in a stability in the Stonehenge landscape, a landscape of identifiable settlements with an economy based firmly on mixed farming. It is consequently surprising that there is very little evidence for the continuity of this apparently established pattern beyond the end of the Bronze Age.

Evidence for Iron Age activity within the Stonehenge area ranges considerably in scale, with the most obvious settlement evidence occurring in the eastern half close to the River Avon. Vespasian's Camp, a univallate hillfort (having a single ditch and bank) lies on a prominent spur immediately above a meander of the river. Although undated it probably belongs to the earlier part of the Iron Age. Further north, traces of both enclosed and unenclosed settlement of later Iron Age date have been recorded within and around Durrington Walls. Despite this background evidence, however, the extensive programme of fieldwalking carried out as part of the Stonehenge

Environs project failed to produce a single sherd of pottery of Iron Age date. Beyond the areas of settlement noted above, only sporadic activity has previously been recorded, from Stonehenge itself, and from the upper levels of the Wilsford Shaft.

In the absence of accompanying dating evidence the environmental background for this period is difficult to determine, although available data indicates that the extensive areas of both arable and maintained grassland which had developed by the later Bronze Age were largely maintained, not only in the Iron Age, but throughout the historic period.

The evidence for Romano-British activity suggests a very scattered pattern of small settlements with some, particularly those on Rox Hill to the south and close to Winterbourne Stoke Crossroads, situated within areas of 'Celtic' fields which appear to have originated in the Bronze Age. The most coherent and extensive site is again located close to Woodhenge and Durrington Walls. Fieldwalking to the west of Woodhenge produced substantial quantities of Romano-British pottery and parch marks within the grass fields during 1989 and 1990 showed enclosures, pits and what appear to be associated burials.

The pattern of settlement during the Saxon and medieval periods is focused firmly on the valleys of the Rivers Till and Avon, and it can be assumed that the pattern of valley edge cultivation and downland grazing, evidence for which can be found in post-medieval documentation, was long-established. The extent of the arable fields of the villages of Durrington, Amesbury and West Amesbury could clearly be seen in the distribution of medieval and post-medieval pottery and tile revealed by fieldwalking. Fragments of such durable materials become incorporated within the domestic refuse and farmyard manure, the precious commodities which were carefully collected and spread onto the fields to maintain their precarious fertility.

It has only been within this century that cultivation has spread beyond the boundaries established in the medieval period. The pressures for increased food production, in part generated by the shortages of two world wars, in part economic, have changed the face of the Stonehenge Environs. The downland is gone, replaced in many areas by arable land which nibbles the edges of the surviving barrow mounds. The re-established grassland buffers such survivors but lacks the ecological diversity of the old sheep-grazed turf and the subtlety of the earthworks recorded by Stukeley has gone for ever. Enough survives to tell an eloquent story of the achievements of the past 5000 years. The battered fragments are now treated with a new respect which will ensure their survival into the next millennium and, it is hoped, beyond.

——11——
Stonehenge – beyond the evidence

Part of this chapter will be concerned with the fictitious side of the Stonehenge story, where imagination and invention go far beyond the bounds of the evidence, in many cases to produce works of pure fiction. Stonehenge has appeared with great regularity in such works, the plot in many cases revolving around the construction of the henge and the power struggles and intrigues that this is assumed to have generated in prehistoric society. This chapter is not intended to rival such works as *The Priestess of Henge, Pillar of the Sky* or *Stonehenge, Where Atlantis Died*, but rather to explore some of the areas of speculation and pure myth which arise most frequently in the questions of visitors to Stonehenge.

In chapter 4 I attempted a description of Stonehenge, including its physical form, its approximate age and the sequence in which it was constructed. It is hardly surprising that such bare bones frequently fail to satisfy the curiosity which Stonehenge arouses. Unfortunately the presentation of archaeological data, even when dressed up with a little imaginative spice, often lacks the immediate appeal of the more confident, but in many cases unfounded, interpretations of those who 'understand' the meaning of Stonehenge. No other monument of the prehistoric past has attracted as much theory, interpretation and speculation as Stonehenge, a mass of literary outpourings beyond the capacity of this chapter even to summarize. None of them should be dismissed out of hand, as they all represent the beliefs of those who have taken the trouble to think about Stonehenge and to commit their thoughts to paper. There are, however, certain common themes and some serious conclusions and theories about Stonehenge which merit some further

consideration. Some will be addressed by this chapter.

What did Stonehenge look like when it was new?

There are times during the period of construction when Stonehenge must have resembled a building site, with gangs of workers shaping and erecting stones, clearing away mounds of spoil and tidying up in preparation for the ceremonies for which we assume that Stonehenge was built. Assuming that the ruins that we can see today are those of the complete Stonehenge, we can be reasonably certain of what its bare bones looked like (**104**), if not its complete original appearance. In the same way that a skeleton, without flesh, skin and hair cannot tell us very much of the appearance of the individual, we cannot be certain how much of the flesh has decayed from Stonehenge in the past 3000 years. It may simply have been a temple of austere stone, the sheer scale and novelty of its construction enough to render any ornamentation unnecessary. Alternatively, the stones may have formed the framework for additional wooden structures, a platform for elaborate totems, or may themselves have been brightly decorated. These days we are used to seeing the timber buildings of the Middle Ages framed in dark oak, a sober image that fits well with our conceptions of what 'old' should look like. Look closer and cracks in the timbers reveal traces of bright paint and gilding, suggesting a positively gaudy original appearance. In the same way Stonehenge may well have been lavishly decorated, perhaps not all year round, but only at certain special times. Then the whole interior may have been covered with offerings and the stones garlanded with

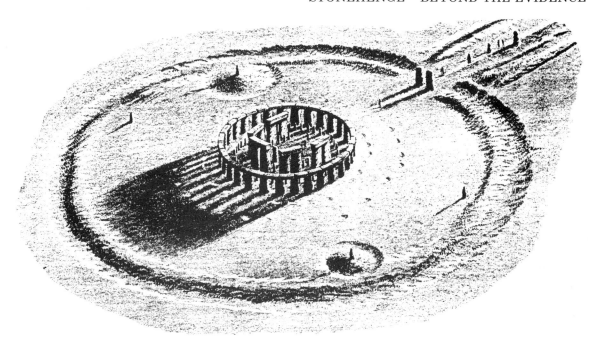

104 *The final Stonehenge.*

blossom, flowers or berries according to season, in the same way that our Christian churches today are filled with produce in celebration of Harvest Festival.

What went on inside Stonehenge?

If we are uncertain about the precise appearance of Stonehenge then we must be equally uncertain about the nature of the ceremonies that took place there in the Neolithic and Bronze Age. This is a favoured area of speculation, with the centre of Stonehenge suggested as a place for marriage, sacrifice or as a place where the bodies of the dead were exposed for a few hours or a few days prior to their burial in the surrounding barrows. None of these can be proved, none would have left any recordable trace even if the centre, where these activities are suggested as having taken place, had not been as disturbed as recent investigations now suggest. To return to the analogy with the Christian church, without knowledge of the basic tenets of Christianity, how many of the elaborate ceremonies, of marriage, christening or communion that are enacted within the confines of the church building could be deduced from its ground plan? In many ways,

in our current state of ignorance about the lives of the people who built Stonehenge, we have little right to put forward our suggestions for its purpose and use, and no right at all to present such suggestions as fact.

Why was Stonehenge built?

The chapter which described the physical layout of Stonehenge noted the re-alignment of the enclosure entrance and the building of the first stage of the Avenue on the same alignment. This alignment, which marks sunrise at the midsummer solstice, is shared with that of the entrances of both Woodhenge and Coneybury, and with other similar monuments much further afield. This concern with a major calendrical event, the longest day of the year, a concern which is strong enough to warrant the building of great communal structures, seems quite reasonable for people whose subsistence was based increasingly on agriculture.

The overall alignment cannot be denied, but its most frequently suggested emphasis, on the midsummer sunrise, can be questioned. Much depends on our perceptions of the use of the space within Stonehenge, traditionally viewed as somewhere to look out of on 21 June with the sun rising over the Heel Stone. The alternative is to look *into* Stonehenge on 21 December, either from the entrance or from the open side of the horseshoes, when the view is of the midwinter sun setting between the two uprights of the great trilithon. Perhaps this annual event, the shortest day of the year, would be more significant to these agricultural communities, as it marked the time of year when the days would begin to lengthen. As the hours of daylight increased from this turning point onwards the certainty would grow that the seasons were going to follow their natural order, spring would come after winter, crops would grow and life would go on as before.

This is a somewhat simple solution, and is insufficient for many who wish to see a greater complexity within Stonehenge: but it is not to deny that such complexity may exist.

Was Stonehenge built as an astronomical observatory?

Stonehenge is in many ways what you wish to make of it. To Alexander Thom, his meticulous measured survey of Stonehenge in 1973 provided evidence of a sophisticated geometrical construction involving spirals, true circles and elliptical settings. Calculations suggested the use of a standard unit of measurement, the 'megalithic rod' (1 megalithic rod is equal to $2\frac{1}{2}$ megalithic yards, each of 2.72 ft). The results of this study, and of many others at sites from northern Scotland to the alignments of Carnac in Brittany, make many claims for their builders. Standard measuring units and the use of geometric shapes, many based on Pythagorean right-angled triangles, imply a level of sophistication perhaps out of place within the societies of this time.

The claims of astronomy are equally demanding of the attention of the archaeologist, who finds it necessary to grasp the principles of another discipline in order to make any kind of fair assessment. Since the original discoveries of Sir Norman Lockyer, Gerald Hawkins, Fred Hoyle and Alexander Thom, aided in recent decades by the analytical power of the computer, have added their more reasoned interpretations to the great astronomical debate. The majority of the recent theories involve the movements of the sun, a straightforward annual cycle, and the more complex movements of the moon which necessitate observation over a period of nineteen years. With patience twelve major directions of the sun and moon can be ascertained and the debate over the astronomical significance of Stonehenge revolves around the correlation of these direc-

tions with alignments embodied within both the henge and its surrounding landscape. Stonehenge itself provides a considerable number of potential alignment points within the central stones and beyond these the Y, Z and Aubrey Holes together with the outlying Slaughter, Station and Heel Stones. The landscape too, densely crowded with skyline burial mounds, provides many potential foresights for proposed alignments.

Desmond Hawkins' studies, which declared Stonehenge to be a 'Neolithic computer', were published in *Stonehenge Decoded* and showed a pattern of alignments on the twelve solar and lunar directions that would arise by chance with a probability of less than one in a million. This apparently persuasive work is an illustration of some of the uneasiness that exists between archaeology and astronomy, and the reasons for the armed truce which so often seems to be maintained between these two disciplines. Hawkins was not the first to be uncritical of the evidence that he was using, putting together elements of Stonehenge that archaeology had demonstrated could not have been visible at the same time, and even, where useful, incorporating features proven to be of widely-differing date. Many of the suggested astronomical schemes involve the large pits or post-holes recorded in the car park, dated by radiocarbon to the Mesolithic period, and Thom's long-distance lunar foresights incorporate skyline features of demonstrably modern date.

The arguments for and against the deliberate construction of Stonehenge for astronomical purposes are long and complex, and only a tiny fraction has been outlined above. The great volume of evidence presented in favour of astronomy in many ways serves to argue against its own cause. There are so many schemes, all apparently plausible, and yet all of which cannot have existed simultaneously. In brief, Stonehenge is far removed from the modern concept of an observatory, with its high scientific overtones. Instead it may mark the beginnings of an astronomical awareness, perpetuating in stone records made over a considerable time, of the patterns of movement of the sun and the moon. The needs of the Neolithic and Bronze Age farmers have already been suggested and, as Christopher Chippindale has noted in concluding his chapter on this very subject: 'Simple calendars, simple divisions of the solar year are more likely than abstract science to find themselves monumentally commemorated in Stonehenge.'

What have the Druids got to do with Stonehenge?

The short answer is nothing. The Druids of historical reality were an Iron Age priesthood, about whom we know little beyond the description of the Roman historian Tacitus writing in about 60 AD. He records the shrieking dishevelled priests who confronted the Roman troops on the island of Anglesey and says that after battle they would 'shed the blood of their prisoners on their altars and consult their gods over the reeking bowels of men'. Pliny describes less harrowing scenes of worship in natural groves, centred on the sacred oak tree and with a great reverence for misletoe. Not only were the Druids nearly a millennium late for even the latest use of Stonehenge, but their preference for places of worship did not apparently include stone structures in a largely treeless landscape.

John Aubrey was responsible for the introduction of the Druids to Stonehenge, but was followed quite happily by subsequent antiquarians, particularly William Stukeley (see **21**). The publication of *The History of the Religion and Temples of the DRUIDS* in 1740 set the seal for their totally spurious association with Stonehenge which has persisted to the present day and which looks likely to persist in the future.

What is Stonehenge?

Stonehenge should best be regarded as a prehistoric temple, its scale of construction raising it far above the many other monuments constructed for a similar purpose. The temple is set within an immediate area originally of great significance, from which everyday activities may have been excluded. Only beyond this can we see the cemeteries and further still the dwellings of the builders and worshippers. This is the same pattern which can be seen in the medieval city of Salisbury, where the great medieval cathedral is separated from the town by the clear expanse of the Close. Here, instead of rich burial mounds at the junction between the religious and the commercial, we see rich houses. It is easier for us to understand the motivation behind the construction of a great cathedral, the power of medieval Christian faith providing the contrast between the soaring spire and the more lowly buildings of the medieval inhabitants of the town. The contrast is equally striking at Stonehenge, here between the enduring monument to the beliefs and fears of the prehistoric inhabitants of the Plain, and the humble traces of their settlements.

There is much that we still do not understand about Stonehenge, there is much that we will never understand. As a monument, as a mystery, as a living centre of worship, it will continue to fascinate and inspire. Perhaps we can do no better than to echo the words of Sir Richard Colt Hoare in describing Stonehenge: HOW GRAND! HOW WONDERFUL! HOW INCOMPREHENSIBLE!

Stonehenge today

There is little wisdom in providing a detailed description of the facilities, interpretation and arrangements for access available at Stonehenge in 1991. Considerable changes are planned for the near future and, in consequence, only the more enduring aspects of visiting both Stonehenge and Wiltshire in general will be introduced.

It is unlikely that any future change will reinstate unrestricted access to the centre of Stonehenge, leaving the view of the stones as either that from the path to the west or from the outside of the earthwork to the south and east. Guidebooks present Stonehenge in plan, and show details of the interior, but Figures **105**, **106** and **107** offer explanation of the view that is available to the majority of visitors.

It is possible to explore much of the prehistoric landscape of the Stonehenge Environs that has been described in previous chapters. Woodhenge is open to the public with no restrictions on access, and footpaths within the National Trust Stonehenge Estate offer access to several barrow groups and to the entire length of the Cursus (**108**).

Both Salisbury and South Wiltshire Museum (in The Cathedral Close, Salisbury) and the Museum of the Wiltshire Archaeological and Natural History Society (Long Street, Devizes), have collections relating to both Stonehenge and the monuments within the environs. Salisbury's includes material from Stonehenge itself and the wonderful Grooved Ware pottery from Durrington Walls, while Devizes houses the spectacular barrow finds from the explorations of Colt Hoare and Cunnington.

Julian Richards
11.90

105 *Stonehenge: the view at ground level explained.*

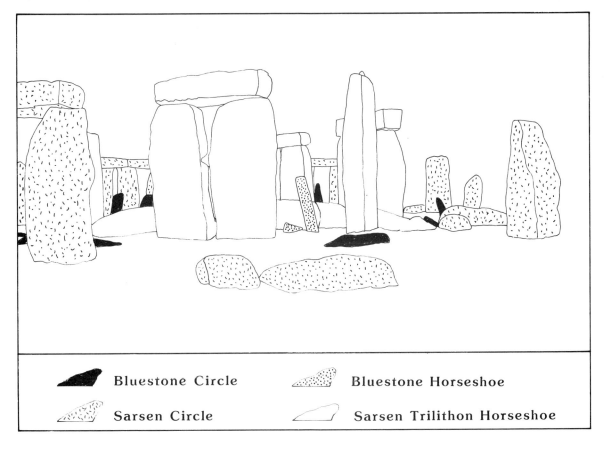

| Bluestone Circle | | Bluestone Horseshoe |
| Sarsen Circle | | Sarsen Trilithon Horseshoe |

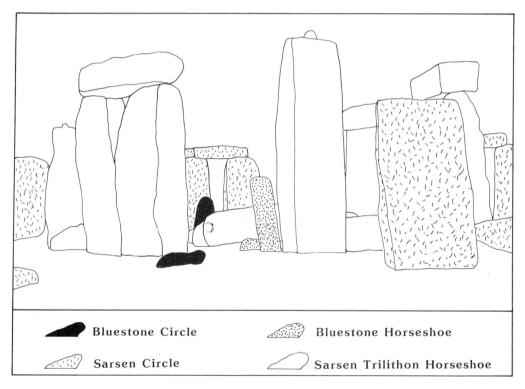

Bluestone Circle		Bluestone Horseshoe	
Sarsen Circle		Sarsen Trilithon Horseshoe	

106 *Stonehenge: the view at ground level explained.*

107 *The position of the dagger carvings.*

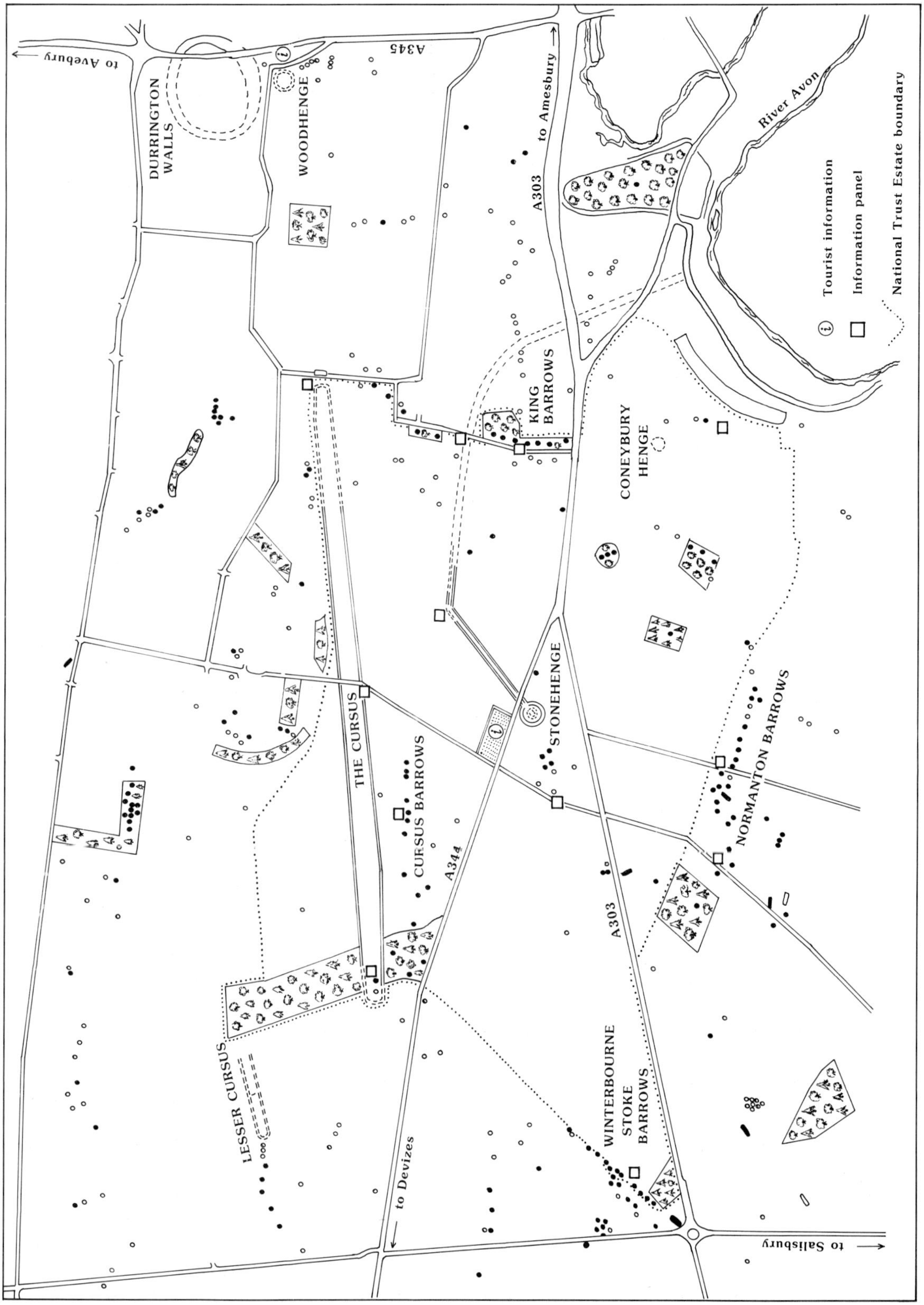

108 *A visitors map of the Stonehenge Environs.*

Further Reading

Essential reading for those wishing to study the Stonehenge Environs in greater depth are:

Royal Commission on the Historical Monuments of England, 1979, *Stonehenge and its Environs*, Edinburgh.

Richards, J. C., 1990, *The Stonehenge Environs Project* English Heritage Archaeological Report no. 16, London.

For a lively over-view of all that is odd and unusual about Stonehenge then read:

Chippindale, C., 1983, *Stonehenge Complete*, London.

For a series of contradictory ideas about Stonehenge:

Chippindale, C. (ed.), 1990, *Who Owns Stonehenge?*, London.

Further more general reading should include the following:

Ashbee, P., Bell, M., and Proudfoot, E., *The Wilsford Shaft: Excavations 1960-62*, English Heritage Archaeological Report no. 11 London.

Atkinson, R. J. C., 1979, *Stonehenge*, London.

—, 1984, 'Barrows excavated by William Stukeley near Stonehenge', *Wiltshire Archaeological and Natural History Mag.*, **79**, 244–6.

Atkinson, R. J. C., and Evans, J. G., 1978, 'Recent excavations at Stonehenge, *Antiquity*, **52**, 235–6.

Bond, D., 1983, 'An excavation at Stonehenge', 1981, *Wiltshire Archaeol. Natur. Hist. Mag.*, **77**, 39–44.

Bradley, R., 1978, *The Prehistoric Settlement of Britain*, London.

Bradley, R., 1984, *The Social Foundations of Prehistoric Britain*, London.

Burgess, C., 1980, *The Age of Stonehenge*, London.

Christie, P. M., 1963, 'The Stonehenge Cursus', *Wiltshire Archaeol. Natur. Hist. Mag.*, **58**, 370–82.

Cunnington, M. E., 1929, *Woodhenge*, George Simpson, Devizes.

Entwistle, R., and Richards, J. C., 1987, 'The geophysical and geochemical properties of lithic scatters', in *Lithic analysis and later British prehistory* (eds. A. G. Brown and M. R. Edmonds), BAR, **162**, 19–38, Oxford.

Evans J. G., 1972, *Land Snails in Archaeology*, London.

—, 1984, 'Stonehenge: the environment in the late Neolithic and early Bronze Age and a Beaker age burial', *Wiltshire Archaeol. Natur. Hist. Mag.*, **78**, 7–30.

Gingell, C. J., 1986, 'A long barrow, Woodford G2, south of Druid's Lodge', in Harding and Gingell 1986, 15–21.

Gingell, C. J., 1988, 'Twelve Wiltshire round barrows. Excavations in 1959 and 1961 by F. de M. and H. L. Vatcher', *Wiltshire Archaeol. Natur. Hist. Mag.* **82**, 19–76.

Gowland, W., 1902, 'Recent excavations at Stonehenge', *Archaeologia*, **58**, 37–105.

Green, C., and Rollo-Smith, S., 1984, 'The excavation of eighteen round barrows near Shrewton, Wiltshire', *Proceedings of the Prehistoric Society* 50, 255–318.

Grimes, W. F., 1964, 'Excavations in the Lake Group of barrows, Wilsford, Wiltshire, in 1959', *Bulletin of the Institute of Archaeology, University of London*, 4, 89–121.

Harding, P. A., 1988, 'The Chalk Plaque Pit, Amesbury', *Proc. Prehist. Soc.*, **54**, 320–7.

Harding, P. A., and Gingell, C. J., 1986, 'The excavation of two long barrows by F. de M. and H. F. W. L. Vatcher', *Wiltshire Archaeol. Natur. Hist. Mag.*, **80**, 7–22.

Hawley, W., 1921, 'The excavations at

Stonehenge', *Antiquaries Journal*, **1**, 19–39.

—, 1922, 'Second report on the excavations at Stonehenge', *Antiq. J.*, **2**, 36–51.

—, 1923, 'Third report on the excavations at Stonehenge', *Antiq. J.*, **3**, 13–20.

—, 1924, 'Fourth report on the excavations at Stonehenge', *Antiq. J.*, **4**, 30–9.

—, 1925, 'Report on the excavations at Stonehenge during the season of 1923', *Antiq. J.*, **5**, 21–50.

—, 1926, 'Report on the excavations at Stonehenge the season of 1924', *Antiq. J.*, **6**, 1–25.

—, 1928, 'Report on the excavations at Stonehenge during 1925 and 1926', *Antiq. J.*, **8**, 149–76.

Hoare, R. C., 1810, *The Ancient History of Wiltshire*, London.

Laidler, B., and Young, W. E. V., 1938, 'A surface flint industry from a site near Stonehenge', *Wiltshire Archaeol. Natur. Hist. Mag.*, **48**, 151–60.

Longworth, I. H., 1984, *Collared Urns of the Bronze Age in Great Britain and Ireland* Cambridge University Press.

Newell, R. S., 1931, 'Barrow 85, Amesbury (Goddard's List)'. *Wiltshire Archaeol. Natur. Hist. Soc.* **45**, 253–261.

Pitts, M. W., 1979-80, 'On two barrows near Stonehenge', *Wiltshire Archaeol. Natur. Hist. Mag.*, **74–5**, 181–4.

—, 1982, 'On the road to Stonehenge: report on the investigations beside the A344 in 1968, 1979 and 1980', *Proc. Prehist. Soc.*, **48**, 75–132.

Richards, C., and Thomas, J., 1984, 'Ritual activity and deposition in later Neolithic Wessex', in *Neolithic studies* (eds. R. Bradley and J. Gardiner), BAR, **133**, 189-218, Oxford.

Richards, J. C., 1985, *Beyond Stonehenge*, Salisbury.

Smith, G., 1973, 'Excavation of the Stonehenge Avenue at West, Wiltshire, *Wiltshire Archaeol. Natur. Hist. Mag.*, **68**, 42–56.

—, 1979–80, 'Excavations in Stonehenge car park', *Wiltshire Archaeol. Natur. Hist. Mag.*, **74–5**, 181.

Smith, R. W., 1984, 'The ecology of Neolithic farming systems as exemplified by the Avebury region of Wiltshire', *Proc. Prehist. Soc.*, **50**, 99–120.

Stone, J. F. S. 1935, 'Some discoveries at Ratfyn, Amesbury and their bearing on the date of Woodhenge', *Wiltshire Archaeol. Natur. Hist. Mag.*, **47**, 55–67.

—, 1938, 'An early Bronze Age grave in Fargo Plantation near Stonehenge', *Wiltshire Archaeol. Natur. Hist. Mag.*, **48**, 357–70.

—, 1947, 'The Stonehenge Cursus and its affinities', *Archaeology Journal*, **104**, 7–19.

—, 1949, 'Some Grooved Ware pottery from the Woodhenge area', *Proc. Prehist. Soc.*, **15**, 122–27.

Stone, J. F. S., and Young, W. E. V., 1948, 'Two pits of Grooved Ware date near Woodhenge', *Wiltshire Archaeol. Natur. Hist. Mag.*, **52**, 287–306.

Stone, J. F. S., Piggott, S., and Booth, A. St J., 1952, 'Durrington Walls, Wiltshire: recent excavations at a ceremonial site of the early second millennium BC', *Antiq. J.*, **34**, 155–77.

Stukeley, W., 1740, *Stonehenge: a temple restor'd to the British Druids*, London.

Thomas, N., 1964, 'The Neolithic causewayed camp at Robin Hood's Ball, Shrewton', *Wiltshire Archaeol. Natur. Hist. Mag.*, **59**, 1–27.

Vatcher, F. de M., 1961, 'The excavation of the long mortuary enclosure on Normanton Down, Wilts', *Proc. Prehist. Soc.*, **27**, 160–73.

Vatcher, H. L., and Vatcher, F. de M., 1973, 'Excavation of three postholes in Stonehenge car park', *Wilts. Archaeol. Natur. Hist. Mag.*, **68**, 57–63.

Wainwright, G. J., and Longworth, I. H., 1971, *Durrington Walls: excavations 1966–1968*, Report of the Research Committee of the Society of Antiquaries, London, **29**.

Wainwright, G. J., Donaldson, P., Longworth, I. H., and Swan, V., 1971, 'The excavation of prehistoric and Romano-British settlements near Durrington Walls, Wiltshire, 1970', *Wiltshire Archaeol. Natur. Hist. Mag.*, **66**, 76–128.

Glossary

'activity' A very loose term used by prehistorians in an attempt to define the significance of a single post-hole or an amorphous scatter of artefacts found by fieldwalking. The range of activities encompassed by this term is almost infinite.

Beaker Finely-made and usually highly-decorated pottery vessels of the latest Neolithic and early Bronze Age periods. Their introduction into Britain, associated with the first metal weapons and a new type of flint arrowhead, is accompanied by marked shift towards the practice of individual burial under round barrows.

bluestone The name given to the stones within Stonehenge which are linked together by virtue of their geological provenance in the Preseli Mountains in Wales.

Bronze Age The period subsequent to the Neolithic, from c. 2000–800BC. Characterized by the first use of metal (initially strictly copper rather than Bronze), and individual burials under round barrows. The period is traditionally sud-divided by means of ceramic and metalwork styles.

causewayed enclosure Sometimes known as an 'interrupted ditch enclosures', the appearance of the one, two or occasionally three circuits of ditch and bank is very much like a string of sausages. Traditionally regarded as places of 'meeting' at which gift exchange and feasting would take place, each excavation which takes place on sites of this type suggests that a wider range of functions is possible. Alongside those already mentioned these may include defence, everyday settlement, and the exposure of corpses prior to burial.

'Celtic' fields The small, rectangular fields characteristic of the first truly intensive arable use of the chalk. This is likely to have been some time during the Bronze Age. The fields consist of cross-slope banks (lynchets) and downslope elements, often slighter in profile.

crouched burial The burial position, often described as foetal, preferred during the Neolithic and Bronze Age periods. The tightly-crouched position of some suggests that bodies may have been bound up into such a position before burial.

cursus An elongated, rectangular, ditched and banked enclosure, often with larger banks at each end. Constructed during the middle part of the Neolithic period (c.3500–3000 BC) their function is far from certain and they consequently tend to be regarded as ceremonial (see ritual).

fieldwalking More accurately referred to as 'surface collection'. A survey technique, much used in the search for prehistoric settlement sites, which involves the systematic collection and analysis of artefacts from the surface of ploughed fields.

flint A hard rock which consists of almost pure silica. It is found in both rounded nodules and flat seams and has been widely exploited for tool manufacture since the earliest prehistoric periods. Although it is abundant in chalk areas and within many gravel deposits, surface flint may be flawed by frost action making it unsuitable for certain types of tool.

geophysical survey The overall term for a range of investigative techniques involving the surface measurement of variation in the

GLOSSARY

magnetic or resistance properties of soils. Such techniques can reveal the existence of ditches or pits, the soil filling of which may show a measurable contrast to that shown by the surrounding undisturbed subsoil.

Grooved Ware Elaborately decorated Late Neolithic pottery, associated most frequently with henge monuments where it may have had a ceremonial use.

henge The term applied to enclosures, many of which have a deep ditch and an external bank. Their central enclosed area frequently incorporates circular settings of either timber (Woodhenge/Durrington Walls) or stone (Stonehenge) uprights. They vary considerably in size and although exhibiting some unifying characteristics, may have been constructed for a variety of functions.

long barrow An elongated earlier Neolithic burial mound, early examples of which often incorporate complex collections of human remains. Later, and often shorter, examples, appear to have been constructed for paired or individual burials.

lynchet A cross-slope field boundary formed by the gradual accumulation of soil moving downhill due to processes of erosion associated with arable cultivation. Soil will build up against any boundary such as a hedge or fence, forming a 'positive lynchet'. Down-slope the effects of ploughing are to cut away the slope, forming a 'negative lynchet'.

megalithic The term used to describe constructions using large stones.

Mesolithic The Middle Stone Age, from *c.* 10,000 BC to *c.* 4000 BC, during which a mobile hunter-gatherer economy was practised over the entire British Isles.

Neolithic The New Stone Age, from *c.* 4000 BC to *c.* 2000 BC, a period during which the mobile economy of the preceding Mesolithic period was gradually replaced by agriculture and animal husbandry. The increasingly settled way of life also involved the construction of communal monuments such as **causewayed enclosures, long barrows** and **henges**, while

changes in domestic life can be seen in the first use of pottery and of ground flint and stone tools.

Peterborough Ware The term given to a range of stylistically varied forms of decorated Neolithic pottery, many of the forms of which develop from the simple round-bottomed vessels of the Early Neolithic

radiocarbon (or C14) dating A method of scientific dating that can be applied to any substance that was once living. In archaeological terms this generally means charcoal, wood, bone or antler. All such living organisms contain carbon, including carbon 14, a radioactive isotope. The level of this isotope begins to decrease as soon as the living organism dies, and the amount remaining, when measured in a counter, will give an estimate of the object's age. Radiocarbon dates, expressed as years bc, need subsequently to be calibrated against a calendar derived from samples of known date in order to produce a calendar date, expressed as years BC. All dates shown in this volume are calibrated.

ritual The term used to describe monuments or activities which appear to have no strictly logical function, and which often involve the expenditure of large amounts of organization and labour, for no apparent purpose.

round barrow The overall term used to describe the wide variety of circular burial monuments which characterize the funerary record of the Bronze Age.

sarsen A hard sandstone rock which formed above the chalk about 30–20 million years ago. In composition it is sand, fused together with silica, the substance of which flint is formed.

trilithon A structure made up of three stones: two uprights and a horizontal lintel. Three trilithons still stand within the sarsen horseshoe at Stonehenge.

Wessex Culture The overall term applied to the rich and powerful early Bronze Age warrior aristocracy identified from the finds in their spectacular graves.

Index

(Page numbers in **bold** refer to illustrations)